LIFE'S BIGGEST QUESTIONS WORKBOOK

by
Paul Tice

THE BOOK TREE
San Diego, California

ISBN 978-1-58509-145-4

Cover Images:

main front cover image copyright by Ase

mountain meditator copyright by Rudall30

child gazing at moon copyright by Angela Waye

back cover image, stargazers, copyright by Dudarev Mikhail

Cover layout by
Mike Sparrow

Published by

The Book Tree
P O Box 16476
San Diego, CA 92176
www.thebooktree.com

We provide fascinating and educational products to help awaken the public to new ideas and
information that would not be available otherwise.

Call 1 (800) 700-8733 for our FREE BOOK TREE CATALOG

Dedicated to

Oprah Winfrey
and the guests of Super Soul Sunday
who have continued to ask, and answer,
life's biggest questions

and to Vicki Rider
who has encouraged me
to keep asking them for myself

Also by Paul Tice

Shadow of Darkness, Dawning of Light: The Awakening of Human Consciousness in the 21st Century and Beyond

Triumph of the Human Spirit: The Greatest Acheivements of the Human Soul and How Its Power Can Change Your Life

THIS Is a Book: Why Real Books are Better

That Old-Time Religion: The Story of Religious Foundations, with Jordan Maxwell and Dr. Alan Albert Snow

A Booklet of Meaningful Quotes

Contents

1. What do you think happens when we die?

2. Is there such a thing as reincarnation? Explain why or why not.

3. If reincarnation is real, why are there so many more souls in the world today?

4. Where were people before they were born?

5. Do you believe that some people can communicate with those who have passed on? Explain why or why not.

6. Do you believe in karma – that your actions can affect your future in this life or a
   future life in a similar way? Explain why or why not.

7. Why is there evil in the world?

8. Who or what defines good and evil?

9. If you knew you would die tomorrow, what would you do today?

10. Is a "wrong" act okay if nobody ever knows about it?

11. Finish this sentence and explain why: If I had massive financial wealth, I would…

12. Finish this sentence and explain why: The greatest thing I value is…

13. Is trust more important than love?

14. How do you define God?

15. If you could ask God one question, what would it be?

16. What is the most important thing about God that you would like to share with
    other people?

17. What is the best way you have found to experience God?

18. Is mankind a sophisticated animal that is evolving physically, or a spiritual
    being evolving spiritually? Or both? Explain.

19. Where are we going as a species?

20. What is the best thing we can do to lessen human suffering?

21. Will we finish destroying this planet, or is there a way we can stop it from happening? If you believe there's a way to stop it, explain.

22. When mankind eventually goes extinct, how do you think it will happen?

23. What can mankind do to overcome its hostility toward one another and achieve world peace?

Chapter 5
HUMAN ORIGINS

24. How do you think humankind first began on Earth?

25. The structure of DNA appears to be intelligently designed so, in your opinion, what are the implications?

Chapter 6
HUMAN POTENTIAL

26. It is said that we use only about 12% of the human brain. Why do you think this is so?

27. Does the Law of Attraction exist? If so, how does it work?

28. When two people experience true love, what exactly is happening?

29. The human body carries an energy known in various cultures as chi, prana, orgone, personal magnetism, vital energy, vril, and a host of other names. What is this energy and how can we use it to help ourselves or others?

Chapter 7
METAPHYSICAL

30. What happens during an out-of-body experience?

31. Do you believe in what is called the Akashic Record – a record of all things stored in some higher realm that we might be able to tap into someday? Explain why or why not.

32. Do you believe in angels? If so, what are they?

33. Do you believe in spirit guides or guardian angels? If so, are they different names for the same thing? Or how are they different?

34. Who or what are ghosts?

35. Do you believe that psychic abilities like esp, psychic readings, or foretelling the future accurately are possible? Why or why not?

36. Is everything really connected at some ultimate physical level? Please explain.

Chapter 8
OTHER LIFE

37. Do you believe we are being visited by an advanced intelligence today? Explain if needed.

38. Do you believe we were visited by an advanced intelligence in the ancient past? Please explain why or why not.

39. If it were announced that we have begun to communicate with an alien race and they may one day wish to visit us, how do you think this would affect our world and you personally?

40. If alien beings picked you up and were planning to take over the Earth, what would you say to talk them out of it? Or would you?

Chapter 9

41. The world's greatest philosopher, Plato, said, "Know thyself." What can you do to know yourself better?

42. When do you feel most at peace with yourself?

43. What one book has had the most profound influence upon you and why?
If it happens to be the Bible don't exclude it – but then stretch yourself, and include another one.

44. What is your greatest joy and why?

45. What is your biggest fear and what can you do to oversome it?

46. What is the best thing that was ever done for you by a stranger or someone who did not know you very well?

47. What is the best thing you have ever done for a stranger or someone you did not know well? Why?

48. What is your main goal in this life? How can you accomplish it?

49. What is the most profound experience you've ever had, and why?

Chapter 10

50. What is the purpose of life (all of life) existing on earth?

51. What is the meaning of human life?

52. What is the meaning of your life?

53. Do we have free will? Explain why or why not.

54. What is true happiness? Does money buy it, or can you be truly happy without it?

55. What is more real – mind or matter? What are your reasons?

56. Is reality just a dream? Explain why or why not.

57. If you could change one thing about the world, what would it be and why?

58. If you could go back in history and witness just one event, with no way to change it and without being seen, what would it be and why?

59. Finish this sentence and expand if you wish: Freedom is…

60. Finish this sentence and expand if you wish: Love is…

84. Finish this sentence and expand if you wish: Light is…

85. Finish this sentence and add more if you wish: Compassion is…

86. Do you believe in the collective unconscious – where certain structures or archetypes of the unconscious are common to us all, to the point where we may be sharing some kind of divine or world mind? If yes or no, please elaborate.

87. How do you stay "awake?"

88. Finish this sentence and add more if you wish: Enlightenment is…

89. Are we being guided as a species to an ultimate destination? If so, explain whom or what is guiding us, and what the destination might be.

Chapter 16

90. What one piece of advice would you offer to a newborn infant?

91. What advice would you give to your younger self?

Chapter 17

92. Who have been your greatest spiritual teachers, and why?

93. What is the best advice you were ever given?

94. Finish this sentence and explain your reasons: I believe…

95. Finish this sentence and expand if you wish: If life is a school, I have learned…

96. What's the lesson that has taken you the longest to learn?

97. Finish this sentence and explain why: I am most grateful for…

98. What is the one thing you know for sure?

99. Finish this sentence and explain why: The main lesson humanity needs to learn is…

INTRODUCTION

Life's biggest questions have been asked for centuries by average people up through the greatest thinkers of their time. Each question presented in this workbook relates to an enduring mystery of great importance or a unique modern issue of today. Each answer has the potential to enrich the life of the reader, which was the criteria involved for choosing each question. Although some of these questions may have been partially answered by modern science, most have remained elusive. This workbook allows the reader to search for these answers directly. It may inspire one to explore new spiritual practices, search out important texts, or discover deeper parts of oneself that reveal important insights.

Some of these questions have gained renewed interest in recent times, being asked by Oprah Winfrey to her guests on a television show called Super Soul Sunday. This is not the official workbook for that show – but it has been partially inspired by it. Each week she has interviewed well-known spiritual teachers from around the world. At the end of each episode she asks them a series of questions, referred to as "Life's Big Questions." Despite the importance of them, it became clear that she and her guests had scratched the surface in the exploration of life's great mysteries. This inspired me to develop a more complete list of questions and present them in this workbook format. Everyone should have a chance to answer life's most meaningful questions. If more people answer them and share their findings, it might one day reveal important truths common to us all, or contribute to new discoveries about ourselves.

In the back of this book my own answers are included as examples for the reader, so they can see how someone else answered a question. I think there's value in that. They are not given as standard, generic answers that I believe the average person would give – they are genuinely mine. I don't mind sharing such personal information because the process was so rewarding. These answers may also provide insights that could be of interest to some. I recommend you not read them until after you have provided your own answers. That is why they are in the back. It was originally planned to do this book with my answers alone, but I soon realized it should not be about me. It should be more about the reader. Everyone should have the chance to explore these questions.

It has been a challenge and a joy in assembling the right questions together and attempting to answer them. Life experience will help. I've done inner work on many levels, became an ordained minister, traveled to ancient places around the world to uncover clues, and did graduate level work in Philosophy to explore what the greatest thinkers knew. The previous books I wrote already asked and answered many of these questions, which my readers may notice, including the definition of God, the soul, and the difference between spirituality and religion, among others. I've spent a lifetime researching and writing on these subjects, which I believe may qualify me enough to present this interesting compilation. With my credentials aside, the main purpose of this book remains clearly intact – being a way for each reader to answer these important questions for themselves.

How the Workbook was Born

Late one Sunday afternoon, after watching the Super Soul Sunday show, I was walking with my dog, Sophia, and reflecting on the questions asked for that day. Then something incredible happened. The answers to some of the questions Oprah asked came flooding through me during the rest of this walk. It was as if the gates to a vault of wisdom suddenly burst open and flooded my mind. The answers kept rushing in as I continued the walk. They were extremely profound – and this both startled and excited me. The knowledge seemed to be coming from somewhere else, almost otherworldly. Was it a deeper part of myself? A spirit guide? My higher Self? This really inspired me. It happened with only a few questions so I could retain the information – and couldn't wait to write it all down. Without this unexpected event the book may never have been written.

Answering these questions is an exciting, revealing, therapeutic, eye-opening experience. After answering the first few, I realized this process was challenging me in numerous ways that I was not expecting. It reveals your true self; it allows you to read your own spiritual fingerprints so that, as you go through the book, they start to make sense on a deep and profound level. Once I experienced this, I quickly realized there was no way the book could be about me alone. It had to include everyone.

Again, don't look at the answers given in the back first if you want to get the most out of this book. Don't be influenced. But comparing answers later could be fun and revealing. You could also compare answers with others in a class or group based on the book. These are the biggest and most important questions of all time, so it requires a lot of thought and reflection. Do not try to breeze through and answer all questions in one sitting. It could take you weeks or even months to finish this workbook, but it will be worth it. Putting the proper care and thought into your answers will cause you to grow. The *Workbook* may also function as a kind of "spiritual notebook" for you. It will allow you to express yourself in a spiritual way, from many different angles. As each angle – or part of yourself – gets filled in, a more complete understanding of who you really are may result. With this process, you may learn more about yourself than most any other form of mental challenge you could encounter. This is a hugely rich and rewarding process. Good luck.

Paul Tice

Chapter 1

THE AFTERLIFE

1. What do you think happens when we die?

_____

_____

_____

_____

_____

_____

_____

_____

_____

_____

_____

_____

_____

_____

_____

_____

_____

_____

_____

_____

_____

_____

2. Is there such a thing as reincarnation? Explain why or why not.

_____

_____

_____

_____

_____

_____

_____

_____

_____

_____

_____

_____

_____

_____

_____

_____

_____

_____

_____

_____

_____

_____

_____

_____

_____

_____

3. If reincarnation is real, why are there so many more souls in the world today?

_____

_____

_____

_____

_____

_____

_____

_____

_____

_____

_____

4. Where were people before they were born?

_____

_____

_____

_____

_____

_____

_____

_____

_____

_____

_____

5. Do you believe that some people can communicate with those who have passed on? Explain why or why not.

_____

_____

_____

_____

_____

_____

_____

_____

_____

_____

_____

_____

_____

_____

_____

_____

_____

_____

_____

_____

_____

_____

_____

_____

6. Do you believe in karma – that your actions can affect your future in this life or a future life in a similar way? Explain why or why not.

_____

_____

_____

_____

_____

_____

_____

_____

_____

_____

_____

_____

_____

_____

_____

_____

_____

_____

_____

_____

_____

_____

_____

_____

_____

_____

NOTES

Chapter 2

ETHICS

7. Why is there evil in the world?

_____
_____
_____
_____
_____
_____
_____
_____
_____
_____
_____
_____
_____
_____
_____
_____
_____
_____
_____
_____
_____
_____

8. Who or what defines good and evil?

_____

_____

_____

_____

_____

_____

_____

_____

_____

_____

_____

_____

9. If you knew you would die tomorrow, what would you do today?

_____

_____

_____

_____

_____

_____

_____

_____

_____

_____

_____

_____

10. Is a "wrong" act okay if nobody ever knows about it?

_____

_____

_____

_____

_____

_____

_____

_____

_____

_____

_____

11. Finish this sentence and explain why: If I had massive financial wealth, I would…

_____

_____

_____

_____

_____

_____

_____

_____

_____

_____

_____

_____

_____

12. Finish this sentence and explain why: The greatest thing I value is...

_____

_____

_____

_____

_____

_____

_____

_____

_____

_____

_____

_____

13. Is trust more important than love?

_____

_____

_____

_____

_____

_____

_____

_____

_____

_____

_____

_____

Chapter 3

GOD

14. How do you define God?

_____
_____
_____
_____
_____
_____
_____
_____
_____
_____
_____
_____
_____
_____
_____
_____
_____
_____
_____
_____
_____
_____
_____
_____
_____

15. If you could ask God one question, what would it be?

_____

_____

_____

_____

_____

_____

16. What is the most important thing about God that you would like to share with other people?

_____

_____

_____

_____

_____

_____

_____

_____

_____

_____

_____

_____

_____

_____

_____

_____

17. What is the best way you have found to experience God?

_____

_____

_____

_____

_____

_____

_____

_____

_____

_____

_____

_____

_____

_____

_____

_____

_____

_____

_____

_____

_____

_____

_____

_____

_____

_____

_____

_____

_____

_____

NOTES

THE HUMAN CONDITION

18. Is mankind a sophisticated animal that is evolving physically, or a spiritual being evolving spiritually? Or both? Explain.

_____

_____

_____

_____

_____

_____

_____

_____

_____

_____

_____

_____

_____

_____

_____

_____

_____

_____

_____

_____

_____

_____

19. Where are we going as a species?

_____

_____

_____

_____

_____

_____

_____

_____

_____

_____

_____

_____

_____

_____

_____

_____

_____

_____

_____

_____

_____

_____

_____

_____

_____

_____

20. What is best thing we can we do to lessen human suffering in the world?

_____

_____

_____

_____

_____

_____

_____

_____

_____

_____

_____

_____

_____

_____

_____

_____

_____

_____

_____

_____

_____

_____

_____

_____

_____

_____

_____

_____

21. Will we finish destroying this planet, or is there a way we can stop it from happening? If you believe there's a way to stop it, explain.

_____

_____

_____

_____

_____

_____

_____

_____

_____

_____

_____

_____

_____

_____

_____

_____

_____

22. When mankind eventually goes extinct, how do you think it will happen?

_____

_____

_____

_____

_____

_____

_____

_____

_____

23. What can mankind do to overcome its hostility toward one another and achieve world peace?

_____

_____

_____

_____

_____

_____

_____

_____

_____

_____

_____

_____

_____

_____

_____

_____

_____

_____

_____

_____

_____

_____

_____

_____

_____

_____

NOTES

Chapter 5

HUMAN ORIGINS

24. How do you think humankind first began on Earth?

_____

_____

_____

_____

_____

_____

_____

_____

_____

_____

_____

_____

_____

_____

_____

_____

_____

_____

_____

_____

_____

_____

_____

25. The structure of DNA appears to be intelligently designed so, in your opinion, what are the implications?

_____

_____

_____

_____

_____

_____

_____

_____

_____

_____

_____

_____

_____

_____

_____

_____

_____

_____

_____

_____

_____

_____

_____

_____

_____

_____

_____

_____

Chapter 6

HUMAN POTENTIAL

26. It is said that we use only about 12% of the human brain. Why do you think this is so?

_____

_____

_____

_____

_____

_____

_____

_____

_____

_____

_____

_____

_____

_____

_____

_____

_____

_____

_____

_____

_____

27. Does the Law of Attraction exist? If so, how does it work?

_____
_____
_____
_____
_____
_____
_____
_____
_____
_____
_____
_____
_____
_____
_____
_____
_____
_____
_____
_____
_____
_____
_____
_____
_____
_____
_____
_____
_____

28. When two people experience true love, what exactly is happening?

29. The human body carries an energy known in various cultures as chi, prana, orgone, personal magnetism, vital energy, vril, and a host of other names. What is this energy and how can we use it to help ourselves or others?

_____

_____

_____

_____

_____

_____

_____

_____

_____

_____

_____

_____

_____

_____

_____

_____

_____

_____

_____

_____

_____

_____

_____

_____

_____

_____

Chapter 7

METAPHYSICAL

30. What happens during an out-of-body experience?

_____

_____

_____

_____

_____

_____

_____

_____

_____

_____

_____

_____

_____

_____

_____

_____

_____

_____

_____

_____

_____

_____

_____

31. Do you believe in what is called the Akashic Record – a record of all things stored in some higher realm that we might be able to tap into someday? Explain why or why not.

_____

_____

_____

_____

_____

_____

_____

_____

_____

_____

_____

_____

32. Do you believe in angels? If so, what are they?

_____

_____

_____

_____

_____

_____

_____

_____

_____

_____

_____

_____

_____

_____

_____

33. Do you believe in spirit guides or guardian angels? If so, are they different names for the same thing? Or how are they different?

_____

_____

_____

_____

_____

_____

_____

_____

_____

_____

_____

_____

_____

_____

_____

_____

_____

_____

_____

_____

_____

_____

_____

_____

_____

_____

34. Who or what are ghosts?

_____

_____

_____

_____

_____

_____

_____

_____

_____

_____

_____

_____

_____

_____

_____

_____

_____

_____

_____

_____

_____

_____

_____

_____

_____

_____

35. Do you believe that psychic abilities like esp, psychic readings, or foretelling the future accurately are possible? Why or why not?

_____

_____

_____

_____

_____

_____

_____

_____

_____

_____

_____

_____

_____

_____

_____

_____

_____

_____

_____

_____

_____

_____

_____

_____

_____

_____

36. Is everything really connected at some ultimate physical level? Please explain.

_____

_____

_____

_____

_____

_____

_____

_____

_____

_____

_____

_____

_____

_____

_____

_____

_____

_____

_____

_____

_____

_____

_____

_____

_____

_____

_____

_____

Chapter 8

OTHER LIFE

37. Do you believe we are being visited by an advanced intelligence today? Explain if needed.

_____

_____

_____

_____

_____

_____

_____

_____

_____

_____

_____

_____

_____

_____

_____

_____

_____

_____

_____

_____

_____

_____

_____

38. Do you believe we were visited by an advanced intelligence in the ancient past? Please explain why or why not.

_____

_____

_____

_____

_____

_____

_____

_____

_____

_____

_____

_____

_____

_____

_____

_____

_____

_____

_____

_____

_____

_____

_____

_____

_____

_____

39. If it were announced that we have begun to communicate with an alien race and they may one day wish to visit us, how do you think this would affect our world and you personally?

_____

_____

_____

_____

_____

_____

_____

_____

_____

_____

_____

_____

_____

_____

_____

_____

_____

_____

_____

_____

_____

_____

_____

_____

_____

_____

40. If alien beings picked you up and were planning to take over the Earth, what would you say to talk them out of it? Or would you?

_____

_____

_____

_____

_____

_____

_____

_____

_____

_____

_____

_____

_____

_____

_____

_____

_____

_____

_____

_____

_____

_____

_____

_____

_____

Chapter 9

PERSONAL GROWTH

41. The world's greatest philosopher, Plato, said, "Know thyself." What can you do to know yourself better?

49

42. When do you feel most at peace with yourself?

_____

_____

_____

_____

_____

_____

_____

_____

_____

_____

_____

_____

43. What one book has had the most profound influence upon you and why? If it happens to be the Bible don't exclude it – but then stretch yourself, and include another one.

_____

_____

_____

_____

_____

_____

_____

_____

_____

_____

_____

_____

_____

_____

_____

44. What is your greatest joy and why?

_____

_____

_____

_____

_____

_____

_____

_____

_____

_____

_____

45. What is your biggest fear and what can you do to oversome it?

_____

_____

_____

_____

_____

_____

_____

_____

_____

_____

_____

46. What is the best thing that was ever done for you by a stranger or someone who did not know you very well?

_____

_____

_____

_____

_____

_____

_____

_____

_____

_____

_____

47. What is the best thing you have ever done for a stranger or someone you did not know well? Why?

_____

_____

_____

_____

_____

_____

_____

_____

_____

_____

_____

_____

_____

48. What is your main goal in this life? How can you accomplish it?

_____

_____

_____

_____

_____

_____

_____

_____

_____

_____

_____

_____

_____

_____

_____

_____

_____

_____

_____

_____

_____

_____

_____

_____

_____

_____

_____

49. What is the most profound experience you've ever had, and why?

_____

_____

_____

_____

_____

_____

_____

_____

_____

_____

_____

_____

_____

_____

_____

_____

_____

_____

_____

_____

_____

_____

_____

_____

Chapter 10

PHILOSOPHY

50. What is the purpose of life (all of life) existing on earth?

_____

_____

_____

_____

_____

_____

_____

_____

_____

_____

_____

_____

_____

_____

_____

_____

_____

_____

_____

_____

_____

_____

_____

51. What is the meaning of human life?

_____

_____

_____

_____

_____

_____

_____

_____

_____

_____

_____

_____

52. What is the meaning of your life?

_____

_____

_____

_____

_____

_____

_____

_____

_____

_____

_____

_____

_____

53. Do we have free will? Explain why or why not.

_____

_____

_____

_____

_____

_____

_____

_____

_____

_____

_____

_____

54. What is true happiness? Does money buy it, or can you be truly happy without it?

_____

_____

_____

_____

_____

_____

_____

_____

_____

_____

_____

_____

55. What is more real – mind or matter? What are your reasons?

_____

_____

_____

_____

_____

_____

_____

_____

_____

_____

_____

_____

_____

56. Is reality just a dream? Explain why or why not.

_____

_____

_____

_____

_____

_____

_____

_____

_____

_____

_____

_____

57. If you could change one thing about the world, what would it be and why?

_____

_____

_____

_____

_____

_____

_____

_____

_____

_____

_____

_____

58. If you could go back in history and witness just one event, with no way to change it and without being seen, what would it be and why?

_____

_____

_____

_____

_____

_____

_____

_____

_____

_____

_____

59. Finish this sentence, then expand if you wish: Freedom is...

_____

_____

_____

_____

_____

_____

_____

_____

_____

_____

_____

_____

60. Finish this sentence, then expand if you wish: Love is...

_____

_____

_____

_____

_____

_____

_____

_____

_____

_____

_____

_____

_____

_____

Chapter 11

THE PLANET

61. Finish this sentence and explain why: The world needs...

_____

_____

_____

_____

_____

_____

_____

_____

_____

_____

_____

_____

_____

_____

_____

_____

_____

_____

_____

_____

_____

62. What is the best thing you can commit to that will make this world a better place?

_____

_____

_____

_____

_____

_____

_____

_____

_____

_____

_____

_____

_____

_____

_____

_____

_____

_____

_____

_____

_____

_____

_____

_____

_____

_____

_____

Chapter 12

RELIGION

63. Is there one true religion? Explain why or why not.

_____

_____

_____

_____

_____

_____

_____

_____

_____

_____

_____

_____

_____

_____

_____

_____

_____

_____

_____

_____

_____

_____

_____

64. Is heaven on earth possible? Explain why or why not.

_____

_____

_____

_____

_____

_____

_____

_____

_____

_____

_____

_____

65. Is hell a fantasy or is it real? Please explain.

_____

_____

_____

_____

_____

_____

_____

_____

_____

_____

_____

66. If your religion did not exist, how would you worship God?

_____

_____

_____

_____

_____

_____

_____

_____

_____

_____

_____

_____

67. What is prayer?

_____

_____

_____

_____

_____

_____

_____

_____

_____

_____

_____

_____

68. Do you believe there was a "fall of man," where an apple was eaten in the Garden of Eden, we fell from grace with God, and were expelled from paradise? If so, were these literal events, or what really happened?

_____

_____

_____

_____

_____

_____

_____

_____

_____

_____

_____

_____

_____

_____

_____

_____

_____

_____

_____

_____

_____

_____

_____

_____

_____

_____

Chapter 13

SCIENCE

69. What is nature?

70. What is time and what is its true purpose?

_____

_____

_____

_____

_____

_____

_____

_____

_____

_____

_____

71. What is consciousness?

_____

_____

_____

_____

_____

_____

_____

_____

_____

_____

_____

_____

72. In a human being, when does consciousness begin?

_____

_____

_____

_____

_____

_____

_____

_____

_____

_____

_____

73. If everything evolved from amoebas in the distant past, why does the world still have them?

_____

_____

_____

_____

_____

_____

_____

_____

_____

_____

_____

74. Where do thoughts come from?

_____

_____

_____

_____

_____

_____

_____

_____

_____

_____

_____

_____

75. Why is the Universe so incredibly large, where does it end, and what do you believe its purpose is?

_____

_____

_____

_____

_____

_____

_____

_____

_____

_____

_____

_____

_____

Chapter 14

THE SOUL

76. What is the human soul?

_____
_____
_____
_____
_____
_____
_____
_____
_____
_____
_____
_____
_____
_____
_____
_____
_____
_____
_____
_____
_____
_____
_____
_____

77. What is the difference between the soul and spirit?

_____

_____

_____

_____

_____

_____

_____

_____

_____

_____

_____

_____

_____

_____

_____

_____

_____

_____

_____

_____

_____

_____

_____

_____

_____

_____

78. Where does the soul reside?

_____

_____

_____

_____

_____

_____

_____

_____

_____

_____

_____

_____

_____

79. Do animals have souls? What makes you believe this?

_____

_____

_____

_____

_____

_____

_____

_____

_____

_____

_____

_____

_____

NOTES

Chapter 15

SPIRITUALITY

80. What is the difference between spirituality and religion?

_____

_____

_____

_____

_____

_____

_____

_____

_____

_____

_____

_____

_____

_____

_____

_____

_____

_____

_____

_____

_____

_____

_____

_____

81. Do you believe that you have a Higher Self, a greater and wiser part of you that observes your life from afar? If so, what makes you believe this?

_____

_____

_____

_____

_____

_____

_____

_____

_____

_____

_____

_____

82. Finish this sentence and explain why: I'm fully in the present moment when…

_____

_____

_____

_____

_____

_____

_____

_____

_____

_____

_____

83. Finish this sentence and expand if you wish: Darkness is...

_____

_____

_____

_____

_____

_____

_____

_____

_____

_____

_____

84. Finish this sentence and expand if you wish: Light is...

_____

_____

_____

_____

_____

_____

_____

_____

_____

_____

_____

_____

85. Finish this sentence and add more if you wish: Compassion is...

_____

_____

_____

_____

_____

_____

_____

_____

_____

_____

86. Do you believe in the collective unconscious – where certain structures or archetypes of the unconscious are common to us all, to the point where we may be sharing some kind of divine or world mind? If yes or no, please elaborate.

_____

_____

_____

_____

_____

_____

_____

_____

_____

_____

_____

_____

87. How do you stay "awake?"

_____
_____
_____
_____
_____
_____
_____
_____
_____
_____
_____

88. Finish this sentence and add more if you wish: Enlightenment is...

_____
_____
_____
_____
_____
_____
_____
_____
_____
_____
_____
_____
_____
_____

89. Are we being guided as a species to an ultimate destination? If so, explain whom or what is guiding us, and what the destination might be.

_____

_____

_____

_____

_____

_____

_____

_____

_____

_____

_____

_____

_____

_____

_____

_____

_____

_____

_____

_____

_____

_____

_____

_____

_____

_____

_____

WHAT I CAN TEACH

90. What one piece of advice would you offer to a newborn infant?

_____

_____

_____

_____

_____

_____

_____

_____

_____

91. What advice would you give to your younger self?

_____

_____

_____

_____

_____

_____

_____

_____

_____

_____

NOTES

WHAT I'VE LEARNED

92. Who have been your greatest spiritual teachers, and why?

_____

_____

_____

_____

_____

_____

_____

_____

_____

_____

_____

_____

_____

_____

_____

_____

_____

_____

_____

_____

_____

_____

93. What is the best advice you were ever given?

_____

_____

_____

_____

_____

_____

_____

_____

_____

_____

_____

94. Finish this sentence and explain your reasons: I believe…

_____

_____

_____

_____

_____

_____

_____

_____

_____

_____

_____

_____

95. Finish this sentence and expand if you wish: If life is a school, I have learned...

_____

_____

_____

_____

_____

_____

_____

_____

_____

_____

_____

_____

_____

96. What's the lesson that has taken you the longest to learn?

_____

_____

_____

_____

_____

_____

_____

_____

_____

_____

_____

_____

_____

97. Finish this sentence and explain why: I am most grateful for...

_____

_____

_____

_____

_____

_____

_____

_____

_____

_____

_____

98. What is the one thing you know for sure?

_____

_____

_____

_____

_____

_____

_____

_____

_____

_____

_____

_____

_____

_____

99. Finish this sentence and explain why: The main lesson humanity needs to learn is...

NOTES

PART TWO

Author's Answers

The original concept for this book was for me to answer the world's most profound questions. It soon became clear that the readers' own answers would be more meaningful than my own, so this workbook was born. My answers are still included to serve as examples, or may be of value to some people. By no means are they intended to be the "right" answers for anyone other than myself.

There are a few questions that I had put a great deal of thought into and had answered more extensively in previous work. After providing brief answers in this book, I've made reference to those works or the website for those wishing further details. Despite the subtle appearance of being plugs for other books, this was done to provide the most complete and thorough answers for readers who may wish to pursue them.

During this process many of your passions, morals, dreams, conflicts, potentials, treasured ideas and deepest feelings about life, yourself and others tend to come to the surface. It's an amazing process. I was a bit self-conscious about sharing it with everyone, as each reader can share their answers with only those whom they choose. I thought to be more conservative and hold back some of my more personal or meaningful answers – but that defeats the purpose. Telling it like it is serves as a good example and may allow others to make the most of the process themselves. Don't hold back. There's treasure to be found.

Chapter 1

THE AFTERLIFE

1. What do you think happens when we die?

The otherworldly part of you – the soul – will return to the place from which it came. It will carry back with it a record of all of your life's experiences and accomplishments. This is why many who have had a near-death experience report having a complete review or "play-back" of their lives. It all goes with you for the purpose of you learning and growing from the life experience. What gains this understanding is the soul, and coming here to experience life in human form has been its goal. What it accomplishes in a physical body is up to you. According to many who have survived a near-death experience, the soul can break free from its physical self. One is often able to look down and see their body below them while experiencing no more pain. They often travel down a tunnel toward a light that they seem to be drawn to, where they are eventually met by friends or family. A life review sometimes occurs and a greater understanding of their life is experienced. Some who return say that it was "not their time," and they were allowed to come back.

Everything you do matters and is better understood on the other side. You are allowed to see how and why your actions were important and how, why and who they affected. A more complete understanding of your life and its purpose will unfold. There is another world beyond this one that exists on a higher vibration than the physical. Only the soul (which is really you) can enter it, and it brings an imprint of your life. This allows you to grow and learn from the life experience. Depending on what was learned (or not learned) determines your next journey into the depths of this world. As far as I know, that is what happens when we die.

2. Is there such a thing as reincarnation? Explain why or why not.

There is no question in my mind about reincarnation being real. There are far too many stories of people recognizing things and knowing things they could have otherwise not known unless they had been there previously, in another life. One of my own examples is that whenever I hear the music of George Frederick Handel there is immediate recognition and it seems like I know every note. Did I play in his orchestra, or was I previously him? I have no musical skills whatsoever, so this is baffling to me. Children seem to recall such events more easily since they are closer to their entrance into this world and may recall previous knowledge more easily. Researcher Ian Stevenson has documented over 2600 cases of children who have recalled past lives. We are, however, not designed to remember previous lives because we are hard-wired into a brain that connects us with bodily senses of the present, rather than the past. The brain dominates the physical realm while the soul is where past life memories are stored. The soul retains memories from previous lives but, in its wisdom, does not normally reveal them to us because new lessons must be learned with each new life.

The soul may sometimes not shed previous life memories. It may carry traumatic experiences into another life or if it felt a certain lesson was left unlearned from a previous life, it may carry that memory over into this one, possibly as a "reminder" for us to finish it. Some past life memories that surface are connected to things left undone or from untimely deaths. The physical body may also carry remanats from past lives. Ian Stevenson has documented numerous cases of people with birthmarks who recall having wounds, often fatal, in the same spot on their bodies in a previous life. Reincarnation could be true for everyone, but the vast majority of us fail to remember previous lives because we have no need for such "reminders." Past life regression therapy can jog people's memories. This process, with a qualified practitioner, has sometimes freed people of problems or phobias that were otherwise not understood but had been carried over from a previous life. I experienced just one past life regression session, which revealed a sudden death at sea during a storm in the early 1500s. When I hit the water during this session, the bitter cold shocked me. I shivered terribly and gasped for air, which explained why I've always avoided swimming in the ocean. Now I understand.

3. If reincarnation is real, why are there so many more souls in the world today?

This argument is often meant to explain away reincarnation, but it comes from a limited perspective. The question is framed from within the context of human consciousness, while not taking into account other forms. Human consciousness is a higher form of consciousness. Those born as humans do not magically appear in the world with a higher consciousness. Consciousness of a soul must grow, over various incarnations, to the point where one may appear as a human. Then humans may have hundreds, if not thousands, of lifetimes. Higher consciousness accommodates higher intelligence, which is why people do not, for example, have the intelligence of ants. However, the world is filled with many who are incarnating as people for the first time. This is why we see such little compassion and wisdom in the world, and why it has so many troubles. Souls are still learning. Granted, that is what we are here for – but so many young souls have rushed into the world to be human, it has created a surplus of many in need of wisdom. Whenever one is complimented on being an "old soul," just remember, there are a great many young ones out there as well.

4. Where were people before they were born?

Before being born we exist as souls, without bodies, which are conscious beings of light that inhabit another realm. This realm contains a process, where souls may cross over – into and out of the lower, dense physical world that we find ourselves in right now. All I know is that this other place exists. I do not know exactly how the process works for us to descend into this world – whether it is voluntary or operates out of a universal karmic "law," however I tend to believe that it is a combination of both. Some have referred to this place on the other side as heaven, but our dogmatic conception of it and what I believe it really is are so far apart, that another name for it might be more suitable. I would not suggest changing it, however, because the idea we have of heaven, despite being imperfect, gives us great comfort.

5. Do you believe that some people can communicate with those who have passed on? Explain why or why not.

In my opinion, some people have demonstrated this ability in an extremely convincing way. If one wishes to dismiss this skill out of hand without doing any research, then that is their choice. However, open-minded individuals only need to watch television shows, Internet videos or read the books of Lisa Williams, John Edward, James Van Praagh, Theresa Caputo and more. Debunkers attack these people on isolated issues without considering the bulk of their material. Time after time, these gifted people reveal details passed on from the other side that would be known only to the person receiving the message and the person now deceased, who is presumably providing the information. This type of information comes through and is meant to be shared to confirm to the recipient that this exchange is real, and is not something that would have been listed on general "name and address" paperwork that is sometimes provided by audience members before a show. Debunkers will sometimes sift through a great deal of impressive examples like this, ignoring them all, in order to find less foundational things that can be attacked. If they find something that could be considered questionable, they will then believe the entire body of work by a psychic must also be questionable. People, in general, fear the unknown. Some will go to great lengths to debunk areas of the unknown so they may remain safely ensconced in their comfort zones. What we must be clear about is that not everyone who claims to have these skills is as gifted as those just mentioned. Some have the true gift and can prove it, while many others experience more limited results or are, unfortunately, charlatans. This gives the skeptics fuel for their fires. With truly gifted mediums, one should also remember that everyone has bad days, with them included. Expecting perfection from anyone is not realistic. Even the spirits they communicate with are not perfect and this world is far from perfect, so we should keep our minds open if we are to learn and progress. The evidence is there if sought out with an open mind.

6. Do you believe in karma – that your actions can affect your future in this life or a future life in a similar way? Explain why or why not.

When one realizes that all things are connected, this idea becomes more plausible. Each action would therefore have its own consequence, without exception. For example, centuries ago the philosopher Lucretius said, "Violence and injury enclose in their net all that do such things, and generally return upon him who began." He was likely referring to events within a single lifetime. However, should reincarnation be real, such a universal law would not necessarily be limited to a single life time frame. Karma affecting ones' future incarnations is a common belief in India. I do not believe in it as strongly as some do in India – for example, in determining one's rank within the caste system – but I believe that personality traits and possibly physical conditions may carry over, in some cases, between lives. My own personal experience with karma involves things done in this life. It works quickly with me. When I've done something that has clearly caused some kind of imbalance, it is not long before a balancing event comes along to rectify it. Bigger, more important events take more time to get handled, but I've noticed that all things eventually do come back around, in some way. To me, there's no question that karma exists.

Chapter 2

ETHICS

7. Why is there evil in the world?

There is evil in the world because reality is dualistic. The physical world relies on opposites, which allows everything to happen – day and night, right and wrong, good and evil. Evil is the most extreme negative within duality. Nothing can be gauged as "good" without knowing evil. Evil is, unfortunately, necessary, hence the term "a necessary evil." Everything needs an opposite to create the context of events. Even our brains have left and right hemispheres to process events for us. Evil constantly has an upper hand in the world. It can strike at any time—more quickly than something that takes time, creativity and planning. Bullets from a gun have taken greatness from this world in an instant—with the assassinations of John F. Kennedy, Mahatma Gandhi and Dr. Martin Luther King, Jr., to name a few. We have the ability to create great wonders and do amazingly beautiful things, which all come from the indelible human spirit. We need to cherish and value the potential of the human spirit to create such goodness in the world, because in an instant it could be gone. Overcoming evil allows the human spirit to soar. A tremendous power of the human spirit exists within us, regardless of the negative forces that can swoop in and snatch things away from us in an instant. Evil is there, but should never deter us. To confront such things and overcome them is character building. It's spiritual work, "soul work," and it is, at least in part, why we are here.

8. Who or what defines good and evil?

The Creator, which is the source of duality, originally had to define good and evil in its broadest sense. The definition of anything can be found in its original blueprint, so the Creator had to be responsible. In a more limited sense, each of us has our own interpretation of good and evil – playing out various scenarios from within each of our individual, conscious selves. It is up to us to interpret good and evil, keeping in mind that we are players on a much larger stage.

9. If you knew you would die tomorrow, what would you do today?

My affairs would be put in order, making sure that what I leave behind would benefit those most deserving and/or closest to me. Answering this question brings the realization that I should not wait to do this, but if it remains undone it would be the first thing on my list. I would otherwise be sure to say good-bye and give my love personally to those closest to me. With this done, I would put my library into the hands of someone who would find it a proper home and keep it together. As a body, it contains one of the most extensive collections of esoteric knowledge in the world pertaining to who we are, why we are here, and where we are going and should be made available to serious researchers. Lastly, I would want to have made a difference. I would make sure the rights to my written works were in the hands of someone with the belief that they should stay in print and continue to be read.

10. Is a "wrong" act okay if nobody ever knows about it?

No, a wrong act is a wrong act, and not good if kept secret. Everything has implications. Just because someone doesn't know about a wrong act one might perform, doesn't mean it fails to affect them (or you) in some way. The fact that something you do could be considered wrong means that you could be a better person by doing something "right" in its place. One must always try to weigh out the difference between a right and wrong course of action in every situation. Before making a choice, one must be sure that a "wrong" act will in fact have negative consequences, making it truly wrong to do. Sometimes a "wrong" act can have positive consequences and is only wrong within a certain context unrelated to your beliefs (like not aiding a criminal would be considered "wrong" by the criminal, who could convince you of the same idea). In general, if an act is punishable by a trusted authority if known about, then it may not be wise to do it. If it is punishable by a lawbreaker or someone without your interests in mind, then going against them and doing something "wrong," could well be the right thing to do. Everyone has a conscience and knowing, deep down, that you have done wrong can affect you, because it never goes away. Making things right clears one's conscience, and often restores well-being, self-confidence and self worth.

11. Finish this sentence and explain why: If I had massive financial wealth, I would…

…try to make this world a better place by doing what I know best. That means I would open a meeting place where the most interesting, cutting-edge researchers can come and share ideas among themselves and with the public. Its main purpose would be to discover definitive answers to many of the questions found in this book. The center would include about a dozen cottages or hotel for the researchers, a lecture hall for them to present their work to the public, an extensive book collection meant for the serious study of mankind which I've spent a lifetime collecting, a book store, and a small museum containing interesting artifacts from around the world. The researchers could share their work with other important researchers in private, study in the library, and present lectures to the public in the lecture hall. This would add to the tourism of the area, attracting those in search of new intellectual adventures or spiritual growth. Maybe branches could result in other places. In addition, I would donate other funds to organizations already involved in making the world a better place.

12. Finish this sentence and explain why: The greatest thing I value is...

...passion. Nothing important happens in our lives without passion. We would be without discoveries, cures, our families, great art, music, modern conveniences, virtually everything of meaning would be lacking if we were without the passion to do it. Perseverance is useless without passion. Genius, creativity and progress of any kind cannot function without the passion to push it forward. It is what shines your light. Passion comes from the soul. It is the "sail" on our ship of life, and keeps each of us on course. Compassion is just one form of passion – when one receives passion it has "come" to you, therefore *come-passion*. It is simply passion directed toward others, expressing concern for others more than being an expression of oneself. So what I value most is all forms of passion. It is soul work.

13. Is trust more important than love?

Nothing is more important than love. If you are expressing or receiving genuine love, you automatically get trust. How could it be any different? It does not work the other way around, so I believe love to be more important than trust. You can be mistaken by thinking that those you trust have love for you. People must sometimes trust others before knowing them, and things do not always turn out well. For example, so-called "coyotes" are hired to smuggle people across the U.S. Mexico border, and people are forced to trust them. There's no love there. Many have died in these situations at the hands of strangers, being put into situations that a loved one would never allow.

Chapter 3

GOD

14. How do you define God?

God is not a single individual who sits up in the clouds and judges your life and actions. God is connected to all and everything. This God-force was once compressed all together – a whole and complete consciousness, but nothing can happen in this state. Absolutely nothing can happen without opposites, which means having other "things" instead of just being whole and complete. Being complete in Himself and without the ability to have any experiences, God had no way of knowing what He actually was, other than love. He therefore fragmented Himself into multiple, almost endless forms of consciousness, quite possibly through the Big Bang, which created a dualistic physical universe and reality itself. When you split something apart that is whole and complete (in this case the original God-consciousness), the result is a set of opposites. That's why this whole world is based on opposites. You've got an opposite for everything—night and day, up and down, good and evil. God is now discovering what He is composed of through an endless array of actions and interactions, being played out through his entire conscious being – now fragmented throughout the universe. Mankind collectively represents the highest form of God's conscious awareness – but we are blind to this fact. We don't know that we are God. We continue to look for Him, out there, not knowing that He is within us. Each separate spark of consciousness found in each person, makes us part of the divine.

This entire consciousness permeates everything in the universe. It takes on endless forms of awareness and intelligence, with love being God's primary essence. God's love is shared among all forms of consciousness because all things are One – all things are connected. Love is the glue of the universe and holds all forms of consciousness together. When you experience God's love you automatically become One with everything. Duality is simply an illusion, staged for us to play out God's conscious journey.

God wishes to return to His state of wholeness, but this time with full awareness. God is becoming fully conscious through the process of duality. Once we – humanity – become fully conscious, God will become fully conscious. The key is for us, His consciousness, to collectively reach the realization of oneness and our identity with God. God cannot magically pull his consciousness back together after it has been fragmented in such a way. The consciousness itself must do the work, and move past the illusion. For example, we must understand that when we hurt others we only hurt ourselves. Any independent and greedy action has its eventual consequence, which will surface and impact its originator with the same negative energy that spawned it. In the same way, when one does something to help others, the eventual results that surface will enrich the originator's life in a similar positive fashion. It's a basic law of the universe that mankind needs to learn along its journey. We do not know all of the reasons why things are playing out in this way, but what is clear is that we are playing a major role in God's own self-realization. So what is my definition of God? In large part, it is us – currently blind and asleep, but slowly awakening.

15. If you could ask God one question, what would it be?

How can I be of the most help to You?, is what I would ask. I believe that we are all part of God, operating within a larger plan. Whatever I can do to further God's plan, based on my skills and capabilities, is what I want to be here for. The real question, however, is How best can I hear the answer?

16. What is the most important thing about God that you would like to share with other people?

I have created something called The God Pact. It explains the common features of God that all cultures share, then gives one the opportunity to become directly involved with their Creator. It is a simple agreement between you and God, but can be hugely powerful in your life and the lives of others. Since you are a *part* of God, rather than apart from God, you could benefit by acknowledging this in a formal way, so it becomes real to you. God is a loving, non-exclusive being that does not promote hatred, terrorism or exclusivity – we are all God's children. The God Pact works with individuals or groups of any size, and can serve as your personal stand and statement against terror. It could eventually become a positive movement. It is not a company, does not collect money and does not keep track of who signs up. Just read about it, consider it, sign it if you agree, and pass it on. It has the potential to make a positive change in ones' life and in the world. Just go to www.thebooktree.com in the blog area, or see it in my previous book *Shadow of Darkness, Dawning of Light*. What Gandhi describes below is a reflection of its' general aim.

> *We may not be God, but we are of God even as a little drop of water is of the ocean. Imagine it torn away from the ocean and flung millions of miles away; it becomes helpless, torn from its surroundings, and cannot feel the might and majesty of the great ocean. But if someone could point out to it that it was of the ocean, its faith would revive, it would dance with joy and the whole might and majesty of the ocean would be reflected in it.* —Mohandas K. Gandhi

17. What is the best way you have found to experience God?

For me it is meditation. Deep meditation can put one in tune with God. There are those like Gopi Krishna who have experienced what is called kundalini energy rising up through the spine as a result of years of meditation, which completely transformed their lives. They became more creative, artistic, healed from certain conditions or simply discovered (and then expressed) who they really are. I've never experience a drastic burst of rising kundalini, but have had small tastes – through meditation. There are many different ways to meditate but I am more visual. I therefore use mandalas, which are beautiful, artistic pieces of art that often reflect a smaller version of creation. They usually contain a great deal of intricate symbology and a central focal point. This central point is meant to be the place of focus in one's meditation and is symbolic of the essence of reality and/or you, the meditator. For me, the Shingon School of Buddhism, based out of early Japan, has the best mandalas and produces the most powerful results in my experience of the Godhead.

Chapter 4

THE HUMAN CONDITION

18. Is mankind a sophisticated animal that is evolving physically, or a spiritual being evolving spiritually? Or both? Explain.

We are clearly both. As sophisticated animals we still maintain instinctual behaviors of aggression, mating, and are highly territorial. We protect and take territory just like most animals do for the purpose of better food sources, shelter or other valuable commodities. Fossil records show various stages of mankind's development, including a continual increase of the brain case and gradual upright walking. This evolutionary process, as with all physical evolutionary processes, unfolds in a very slow way. It's part of nature and we are part of nature in the physical sense – with animal bodies, all of which have hair, as animals do, and rely on the same biological needs and processes found in the animal kingdom.

Something about this animal-related predicament, however, disturbs us. The spiritual part of us doesn't like animal hair. Most men shave it from their faces despite it being a completely natural feature, and women try to eradicate it from virtually every part of their bodies. This behavior is just one example of the spiritual part of us talking. Something deep down inside of us is *not* an animal and does not want us acting, smelling or even looking that way. But acting like barbaric animals remains one of our biggest challenges and we have slowly, over the centuries, evolved spiritually a bit further away from this. We no longer throw people to the lions like in ancient Rome, or publicly burn people at the stake for having different religious beliefs. We are in general becoming more tolerant and understanding. I believe this is because we are evolving spiritually and slowly awakening. We are somehow composed of both spiritual and physical elements – and both elements are evolving. Our greatness, however, is found in the spiritual part of us. It is the more important part of us because it is who we really are. First and foremost we are spiritual beings. Even Jesus seemed to recognize this. He said in *The Gospel of Thomas*:

> If the flesh has come to be because of the spirit, it is a wonder, but if the spirit has come to be because of the body, that is a wonder of wonders. But I wonder how such a great wealth has come to dwell in this poverty.

Things in the physical world, including human bodies, operate at a more dense vibration that the spiritual. Therefore, they evolve more slowly. Our spiritual evolution seems to be happening at a much faster rate.

19. Where are we going as a species?

I believe we are on a path of awakening, and the result of this awakening will eventually bring us back to God or God-consciousness. There are so many human frailties and obstacles in our way, however, that a huge challenge confronts us on this journey. The power of the mind and human ingenuity has advanced much further than our spiritual awareness. We are groping around with great intelligence in spiritual darkness, believing that our scientific and technological advances hold the keys to our future. They do not. We must consider, for example, the words of Albert Einstein who once said, "Our entire much-praised technological progress, and civilization generally, could be compared to an axe in the hand of a pathological criminal." This is why a spiritual awakening is needed – we are out of balance with the world because we are out of balance with our true spiritual nature. Chaos is the result. The biggest problem we face is that we are currently passive about overall change, content to remain in this crumbling paradigm. We must act before we can awaken. The destiny that awaits us is a *potential*, and it will never happen by itself if we cling to this passive attitude. Our involvement is needed to push the process forward. Many of us do sense that something is wrong. It does not take a genius to see that the path we are on does not bode well for our future if it remains the same. If we should exhibit enough wisdom as a species, then this new direction should contain the following features, as outlined in my previous book, *Shadow of Darkness, Dawning of Light*.

1) Identity. Having an understanding of who we really are and why we are here in the physical world. For example, we are blind to the fact that we are spiritual beings. Without this foundational starting point, it's unlikely that any of the other features will follow or, if they do, have much impact.

2) Education. A completely revised and updated educational system must be based on the revelation of identity. With a better understanding of exactly what a human being really is, we can then intelligently approach how to determine our values and future actions. Greed and materialism should slowly erode as a result. This revelation of identity will not happen overnight, so we should have enough foresight to begin using spiritually-based educational programs ahead of time, to serve as catalysts for higher awareness.

3) Holistic Awareness. Requires us to implement what we have learned through this new educational process with committed action – first locally, then regionally, then throughout the world. This means achieving higher ethical standards, with compassion and mutual respect for other belief systems and forms of life. It also concerns a new ecological, green-based view of the environment, which is already here and beginning to strengthen.

4) Economic Restructuring. Completing this new consciousness, on a worldly scale, involves using the fruits of this gradual awakening in local and world economics. Without such usage, we will remain as slaves. The vast majority in the world could still reach these three previously stated goals or realizations; but if those who control the economic purse-strings of the planet insist on continuing to impose their unawakened materialistic control on the rest of us, then positive change may remain difficult. It does not seem likely that the world economic system will change unless the first three points mentioned are successfully addressed. The first three are a prerequisite for the fourth; otherwise, a successful economic restructuring will likely never be achieved. We can, however, overcome each of these four challenges

with clear focus and intent. Using a plan of this nature can give us control over our destiny, rather than allowing control to be fought over by interests that continually surrender it to one another so that at the end of day, no real progress is made. So where are we going as a species? We are on a path back to God – but need to be aware of it and act on it responsibly if we are to make the journey a success.

20. What is best thing we can we do to lessen human suffering in the world?

Many would look to Buddhism for answers to this question, as this religion has addressed the problem for centuries with the most focus and concern. But since the world would never willingly convert to Buddhism, thereby spreading this concern, we must look elsewhere for a solution. Before we can make any substantial impact on suffering we would have to create an entirely new paradigm first, which involves a worldwide economic restructuring. Suffering will always be a part of the world and we will never eliminate it completely. It is part of life and part of nature. But we can lessen its devastating impact. A new economic structure will occur only from a new way of collective thinking – but thinking in new ways does not change things by itself. People must go beyond thinking about it and *act* in entirely new ways to reflect those new ideas. Less suffering can only be achieved by having a new economic structure in place that is geared toward compassionate action. The world economy we have now is flawed and disintegrating. A new economic framework that rewards compassionate service would therefore allow suffering to decrease.

21. Will we finish destroying this planet, or is there a way we can stop it from happening? If you believe there's a way to stop it, explain.

When it comes to the balance of nature, this earth is populated by ignorant sleepwalkers who continually fight and kill each other over the planet's resources. The "victor" that emerges with control of these valued resources has won the privilege to blindly pollute our home and ruin the fragile, natural balance of the earth. That balance has weakened to such an alarming level that we are in peril of losing our place on this planet should we not make immediate changes. In the past hundred years, we have managed to deplete and ruin millions of years' worth of the earth's precious resources, including much of its water and atmosphere, directly contributing to the extinction of a few hundred thousand species of plants and animals. From a collective level, very few seem to care, or have not bothered to notice. This situation is similar to the Titanic tragically hitting its deadly iceberg, followed by the captain announcing that it's time to take a nap. We need to start acting quickly to reverse some gigantic trends, but it's not going to happen until more of us "wake up." This is no time to take a nap—or rather, to continue it. Survival is about awareness. And with a limited awareness, our priorities – as caretakers of the earth – have become scattered and confused. We can marvel at the incredible technology and amazing scientific advances we have achieved, and base our views of consciousness on that, but we have yet to place them into a larger framework that allows us to function holistically. Our best science and technology are most often used for warfare, the most divisive and damaging human endeavor ever conceived. And we call it progress. I do not know for certain if we will finish destroying the planet or not, but I do know what it would take to stop it. A massive wave of holistic awareness needs to engulf the planet. We should start by reforming the education process on all levels and be sure to include holistic awareness as a central theme.

22. When mankind eventually goes extinct, how do you think it will happen?

I really don't believe our extinction will be from our own doing. I think we will wake up in time to save things and that process is now in full swing. We may have some serious setbacks that would be disastrous, but they will not wipe us out completely. What will ultimately wipe us out will be the same thing that did the dinosaurs in – a large comet or asteroid strike.

23. What can mankind do to overcome its hostility toward one another and achieve world peace?

This is a hard question because the answer, no matter how it's approached, is far away. First, it should be clear that our hostile nature is just that – part of our nature – so we'll never be rid of it completely. But as we mature as a species, we'll be able to lessen the extent of its damage. It would take a number of decades, but the greatest chance for a more peaceful coexistence with one another lies in our ability to either 1) create an entirely new paradigm based on higher principles or 2) unify most of the world under the active recognition of an all-loving God. I cannot claim to hold the answers to the world's problems, but with both of these approaches I have presented, in previous works, an effort to do so. The four-point plan for a new paradigm as found in *Shadow of Darkness, Dawning of Light*, would take decades to unfold, and I am merely an amateur with ideas that could be too basic. But The God Pact could be realized more quickly, which aligns people with an all-loving God. Terrorism is a serious, growing problem and The God Pact has the potential for groups and individuals to pledge themselves against it. It gives each person a voice against all violence toward others, whether it be schoolyard bullying, domestic violence, inner city crime or worldwide terrorism, instead of sitting helplessly on the sidelines. As crazy and far-fetched as both of these things might seem, it wouldn't hurt to try them.

Chapter 5
HUMAN ORIGINS

24. How do you think humankind first began on Earth?

I believe the more primitive versions of us found in the fossil record have evolved naturally, just like everything else in nature has evolved. It is so far back in history that anything beyond using "Occam's Razor," becomes more of a stretch. You have to go with what is the most likely scenario when little proof exists to counter what the most likely answer would be. Beyond this original appearance, millions of years and a few evolutionary jumps in progression later, we became separate from nature and another phase, or "creation" of man occurred. It is often pointed out that there are two creations referenced in Genesis in the Old Testament. So what we are talking about here, in relation to this question, is the first creation. I believe that an immense intelligence is behind the natural world. This intelligence set the world into natural motion but is not directly involved beyond that in any physical way. In looking at the big picture, this reality cannot simply be a random process. The overall design cannot possibly be random. Then we came along in today's form and began making our own clever little designs within this larger framework. When our own designs seem to replace nature's intelligence or even work to damage and deplete it, we as a species may fool ourselves into believing that we are in control and there is no underlying intelligence. But that intelligence is what made us and the world. We did not even appear on Earth until millions of years after nature was set in motion, and we were originally part of nature when we appeared. Despite our advanced evolutionary status, we began as animals on the Earth just as all other mammals have. That's a fact. There may be something else within us that doesn't like this fact, but it is a fact nonetheless.

25. The structure of DNA appears to be intelligently designed so, in your opinion, what are the implications?

When one looks deeply into the overall structure of things, there can be no denying that there is some kind of all-encompassing intelligence behind the processes involved with life. Therefore, it is no surprise to learn that DNA itself, based on certain clues, may have been designed by this same intelligence. When you pop the hood on life, you can see a DNA engine – that's what makes it work. This means 1) All life must have some form of DNA to operate and 2) If you make any changes in the structure of DNA, it also changes the actual entity connected to the DNA. The implications to this are twofold. First, if DNA is intelligently designed there must have been a creator. And two, any highly intelligent beings, whether the original creator or not, would then have the capability to manipulate life forms should they understand the basic DNA structure. Mankind has already misused or tampered with this through the genetic manipulation of crops and animals worldwide. But a bigger question is whether mankind's DNA has itself been tampered with. Scientists have traced almost all human DNA back through to other lesser genes, showing how human evolution has built itself upon necessary prior genes, creating more complex ones in the process. However, scientists have discovered 223 genes in human DNA that do not have the required genome predecessors. As I understand it, these genes are completely missing from the evolutionary record. Scientists have since attributed their appearance to bacteria, but in dissecting their structure and importance (by determining their function by spelling out the various proteins they produce), many of these proteins relate to higher physiological and psychiatric human functions, as published in the esteemed journal Nature. The question is, how does a mere bacteria, introduced "sideways" into mankind's evolution, instead of evolving down the normal tree, suddenly bestow such higher functions upon mankind? Unless there was knowledge about it and what it would do from some other higher intelligence that actually inserted it. Random chance could still be an answer, but such higher attributes being merely random events, without any intelligent involvement, reminds one of seating a monkey at a typewriter and waiting for it to type something from Shakespeare. I'm not an expert in genetics and could be wrong – but the entire field knew very little a few decades ago, so we are all just learning about this.

There seems to be other evidence pointing to outside intervention in the early development of mankind. I spent two and half years as a personal cameraman, traveling the world with a gentleman named Zecharia Sitchin, who was a major proponent of this general idea. We gathered evidence on tape at all of the most ancient and interesting archaeological sites and museums throughout the world. Although I did not agree with everything he proposed, I found many of his ideas to be compelling and worth looking into.

Chapter 6
HUMAN POTENTIAL

26. It is said that we use only about 12% of the human brain. Why do you think this is so?

Science states that the brain acts as a filter; probably designed this way so we could process only what we need for survival. We are surrounded by data that many other creatures can perceive – various wavelengths of sound and light that are not discernable to us. They would only confuse us if our brains were allowed to receive and process them. We were originally designed to be part of nature, with each individual species being given the right components to exist in balance with it. Now that we are estranged from nature and manipulate and control it in numerous ways – ignoring her cycles and catering only to our needs – we want even more brainpower. There's a bumper sticker that says, "If you think education is expensive, try ignorance." We are. The 12% of the brain that we do have access to is not being used properly. But we want more – thinking that more brainpower might get us out of the mess we have made of the planet. Here is the real answer: We are still part of nature. We are still connected to her, as everything is connected – far more connected than can be seen on the surface. And in inclusive systems like this – I suppose we should call her Gaia – the main system is aware of what all the other parts are doing. So when we step back, learn how to use our minds holistically rather than strictly for profit, and make some adjustments, the system we are part of may actually allow us to progress, to evolve, and gain more access to our brainpower. However, we must first prove we can do it responsibly and that, I'm afraid, is a very long way away.

27. Does the Law of Attraction exist? If so, how does it work?

The Law of Attraction does exist; that is partly why there has been so much hype about it. Although people want to tap into it for their own personal advantage and countless self-help books claim to offer the key to this access, the Law of Attraction is not a human law. It is a basic, fundamental law of nature. It takes many different forms in nature – through the colors of birds and insects, the smells exuded during mating periods, the mating dances performed instinctively by many species; calls, cries and howls – all of this and more create the backdrop for the overall law to operate. The most important component of life is, of course, its' ability to maintain itself. This important law insures nature of just that – life will carry on. Many will say that the Law of Attraction involves pheromones, which is a chemical put out by most every species that will attract a mate. But again, we also have colors, calls and more that play into it. There is also a modern metaphysical twist put onto the Law that simplifies it by saying that like attracts like. It claims one can project something out there powerfully, with the mind, long enough and forcefully enough, and it will manifest things for your benefit. Nature is not involved, just the mind. I am a proponent of this only to an extent. I do not discount the power of the mind, but I do discount its ability to provide success for everyone in any kind of endeavor just by thinking about it. What I do believe in is visualization. This is what attracts what is wanted – but one must first plan and be ready for action. Only then do you visualize, over and over again, as if you were performing the action perfectly so that when you actually execute, your actions will follow your intention. Greg Louganis used this visualization technique to win multiple gold medals in Olympic diving as well as winning 47 U.S. national titles. The Law of Attraction works only during the time one is engaged in the specific action that will bring the result, rather than the mind doing it all for you. So yes, the Law exists, but requires action to follow focused intent.

28. When two people experience true love, what exactly is happening?

It is an amazing gift to experience true love. It will always be remembered as a significant, life-changing event for those fortunate enough to experience it. It is even more of a blessing for it to happen between two people at the same time, so the feeling is reciprocal. Science might say that certain needs, chemicals and levels of comfort all get met at the same time, but far more is going on because we are far more than mere animals that seek comfort and exude chemicals. True love operates at the soul level. It is a spiritual connection first and foremost. It happens when two souls recognize each other at a deep level and these souls begin to dance. Anyone who has experienced true love will know exactly what I mean. This is where the idea of "soul mates" came about – when people believe there is another half out there that fits only you. I am not a believer in this limited view, but believe that any two souls have the ability to become soul mates with each other if certain vibrations are present, which can cause them to resonate beautifully together. It may also depend on a certain spiritual make-up, where they were previous to this life, or what kind of path they're on today. To try and define true love beyond this modest attempt is futile since it is something that can only be felt (and not pointed to).

29. The human body carries an energy known in various cultures as chi, prana, orgone, personal magnetism, vital energy, vril, and a host of other names. What is this energy and how can we use it to help ourselves or others?

This is our life energy, often called vital force or vital magnetism in the West. Eastern medicine predates Western medicine by thousands of years, offering alternative ways to heal that involve this force, including acupuncture. Thousands of energy meridians in the body form a pathway for this important life energy. When any part of the path gets blocked we can become sick in certain ways, and a good acupuncturist can clear this pathway and restore good health to the body. Yet the West and large pharmaceutical companies almost always prefer that you take expensive pills over using any other means of healing. So one good way this energy is used is an alternative attempt to heal us of certain conditions or improve our health.

The two main proponents of this energy in the West have been the German, Karl von Reichenbach (1788-1869), and Wilhelm Reich (1897-1957). Reichenbach was a notable scientist who performed thousands of experiments. He claimed that 30 to 50% of people were sensitive to the odic force, as he called it, and could therefore perceive it or work with it easily. Not only is there a high concentration of od within the human body but also, according to Reichenbach, it is most prevalent in sunshine, moonlight, crystals, the human hand, chemical processes (in part), and within the spectra of different kinds of light after transmission through glass. Reichenbach also claimed that od was present, to some degree, in everything. This all-pervading scientific view, later corroborated by Wilhelm Reich, is consistent with the most ancient of spiritual views. This vital energy is truly present in all forms of matter, organic or inorganic, which has caused science to advance the notion that life itself, to some degree, is present in all forms of matter. For example, Haeckel asserts that all atoms of matter are capable of perceiving sensation and responding to it.

Reichenbach claimed that at least one in three people are sensitives. Are you? A simple experiment is to have someone extend their arms and hands out against a dark background in a dimly lit room. Look at the fingertips and if you see a non-luminous "energy" flowing from them, then you are quite likely a sensitive.

Water by itself is jam-packed full of life force—in fact, without it we would die. Although water is not alive in the traditional sense, it contains so much vital energy that it provides life to virtually everything on the planet. We are surrounded by vital energy, but because it cannot be seen we remain largely ignorant of its power. It is ever-present in the air all around us, and some of the most powerful secrets of using this force involve breathing in special ways—for example, deep meditative states are achieved this way. The art of Tai Chi involves proper breathing, as well as certain breath and focusing techniques used by athletes.

Practical uses and more demanding experiments for this energy can be attributed to Wilhelm Reich. His researches into what he called the orgone energy were extensive. From his work he concluded that this energy was the creative force in nature. He also uncovered the fact that people maintain a certain rigidity in their muscles, which blocks the movement of emotional energy. He believed that our society was responsible for this rigid but unconscious defensive mechanism, which was causing a major emotional repression, or sickness, in people. This is the same problem approached through acupuncture in the East.

Reich invented an orgone energy motor, an orgone blanket for healing purposes, an orgone accumulator for collecting the energy, an orgone vacuum tube, and what was called a "cloud-buster." The cloud-buster was, in effect, a rainmaker that used this energy. The first time he tested it, July 6, 1953, was in Maine for blueberry farmers who were experiencing a drought. After setting up the instrument in the morning, it was raining that very night.

His orgone accumulator was about the size of a telephone booth and was meant to gather orgone from the atmosphere for closer study. Although he never officially claimed it could heal, it was often mentioned by others that healing of the common cold, cancer and impotence could occur while one sat inside. The FDA soon forced these items out of existence, destroying many, claiming none of it worked. Reich and his foundation were ordered to appear in court on July 26, 1955 to show why legal proceeding should not be brought against them. We as Americans, in this legal system, are supposed to be innocent until proven guilty. In this case, Reich was considered guilty unless he could prove himself innocent to the satisfaction of the court.

On June 5, 1956 the FDA showed up at Reich's lab and destroyed all orgone accumulators. They returned again on June 26 and according to FDA records, burned 251 documents. This was America in the 1950's, not Nazi Germany. Certain freedoms that we are supposed to have were ignored. Reich himself said, as his work was being torched, that his books had been burned in Germany but he never expected it to happen here. He was brought to jail, sentenced to two years, and died soon after of a heart attack at age 60. Since then, little has been done to revive interest in the subject.

This energy has been recognized throughout the centuries by most every culture known to man. Each of us walks around like a battery, carrying this power with us on a daily basis. Most don't even know it or, although they realize "something" is there, don't care to cultivate, enhance or explore it. Its' overall effectiveness still remains a mystery. Maybe when the time is right it can be approached in the proper way.

Chapter 7

METAPHYSICAL

30. What happens during an out-of-body experience?

Also known in short as an OBE. The physical body is left behind and another part of you, the spiritual body, is afforded the opportunity to "travel." This spiritual body is different from the soul (the soul is more of an observer), but is an energy field that surrounds the body.

We don't experience this spiritual self unless, for some reason, it should break free from its physical shell and one may suddenly find themselves "out of the body." According to many experienced out-of-body travelers, should this happen, your spiritual self is still connected to the physical body through what is called the "silver cord." This silver cord allows one to get back to – and back into – the physical body. During its' travels the spiritual body goes to other higher levels, often referred to as the astral plane, so going here is often called astral travel. Other times it may stay here on this physical level and explore other parts of the world. In this event it is referred to as remote viewing. The US government actually trained remote viewers for a time, during the Cold War with Russia. When the program was eventually abandoned it was announced that the program was a failure. Many who were involved have taught or still teach in the private sector.

There is also a group called The Monroe Institute in Faber, Virginia, founded by Robert Monroe, who wrote a few books on leaving the body and what one may expect. His books are highly recommended. I have heard there are ways to induce out of body experiences, but have never tried them. Despite this fact, I've still had it happen a few times. One night while sleeping I left my body and suddenly found myself plummeting through the air off the side of a building – next to someone. I was shocked but at the same time was more focused on this person, whose clothes were flapping loudly in the wind from this fall. Some kind of connection existed between us, although I don't know what it was. Nor did I know how this person got there, but believe it may have been a suicide. I was comforting this person as we were falling in the night, being right with them all the way, and knew this person was experiencing a great deal of mental anguish. It was not physical pain that had put them in this position. Once the ground came upon us I was still there, cradled this person's head in my arms and told them over and over again that everything would be okay now. I assume that in some deep and unknown way, I had a connection to this person and had to be there for them. This was not a dream. While holding this person I could feel the cold cement on my body just as if I were there. I knew without question that this was something I had to do, was glad to do it, yet have never understood anything beyond that. This type of thing had never happened before or since. I suppose you could say that I once served as a temporary angel – and was glad to do it.

31. Do you believe in what is called the Akashic Record – a record of all things stored in some higher realm that we might be able to tap into someday? Explain why or why not.

If the Akashic Record exists I believe it could be nothing other than the mind of God. One can experience God in powerful ways and gain entry into the mind of God while in human form, which has been described as life-changing and "enlightenment," and I do not doubt many of those stories. But past claims about accessing the Akashic Record without having such an enlightening experience have never produced any convincing results, in my opinion. Nothing has been shared by those claiming access that made me jump out of my seat and agree that it had to happen. I do believe that the mind of God does exist and that people have accessed it. However, the enlightening experiences that resulted happened on a different conscious level than one would experience by browsing records in a library or employing normal conscious thought processes. The Akashic Record may exist and I remain open to the idea. I'm just not sure that I believe all the reports from those who claim to have been there.

32. Do you believe in angels? If so, what are they?

I do believe in angels, but they may not be quite what they seem. In no instance has any account of angels in religious texts shown them to have wings. These wings were added by artists to make clear that this is what they were depicting. The term "angel" is defined as being a messenger of God. When angels show up, they usually carry some kind of message or offer comfort. This is what we've come to expect from them, but that is not always the case. Angels are considered to be good, based on our beliefs, but that is not necessarily so. For example, Satan is also an angel and many angels are said to be the warriors of God. From the bible we find:

And there was war in heaven. Michael and his angels fought against the
dragon, and the dragon and his angels fought back. But he was not strong
enough, and they lost their place in heaven. The great dragon was hurled down
– that ancient serpent called the devil, or Satan, who leads the whole world
astray. He was hurled to the earth, and his angels with him.

—Revelation 12:7-9

Those who do good deeds are often told that they are angels, but we might be using the term too freely. Apparently, angels are not only God's helpers, but Satan's as well.

33. Do you believe in spirit guides or guardian angels? If so, are they different names for the same thing? Or how are they different?

I believe that spirit guides and guardian angels are one and the same. The term "guardian angel" is so prevalent in religion that it is used more often than the more accurate description – a spirit guide. The terms are interchangeable. Based on word meanings, however, and what they do, neither one of them may be actual angels. Whatever you choose to call them, they are still good to have around. The guardian angels in the Bible are said to look after people, comfort them, and are even credited with breaking some Christians out of jail. But nowhere in the Bible does it say that everyone has a personal guardian angel. I do believe that we all have at least one spirit guide – not your higher Self, but a separate, concerned entity that watches over you and may be able help in certain circumstances. When I was about eighteen, I drove three or four friends to an outdoor concert about a hundred miles away. The car broke down on our way back, late at night. There were no cell phones back then, and a guy with a tow truck who we never called showed up out of nowhere and then agreed to tow the car all the way back home, about 80 miles, even though we had no money. The driver of the truck said he didn't understand why he even went out that night. Back home, during all this, my mother was worried and couldn't sleep. Then a bright light appeared in her room. The voice of my grandmother, who died before I was born, told her not to worry, and she would make sure I got home okay that night.

34. Who or what are ghosts?

A ghost is a spirit body that gets left behind from trauma or confusion in ones' passing. We have this spirit body now. The body, soul and spirit are closely connected during life. The spirit is the result of electrical charges that are generated between the human body and the soul while they are connected. When the body and soul disconnect in a smooth and natural death, these "charges" will dissipate over time. Following death, the spirit will linger for a time—some longer than others. If the spirit is separated from the body quickly in a traumatic death, then it can become trapped here, unable to "fade out" because the death occurred too fast to properly sever the soul from its body. Therefore, the soul stays connected to the spirit and animates it (instead of the body), having been duped by the trauma to believe the body is still there, or that spirit must be the body. The soul and spirit now stay connected, not knowing what really happened. The result is what we term a ghost. The soul stays connected to the spirit because that is the only way it maintains its connection to the body. And if it still thinks it has a body, not being "told" otherwise, it will naturally keep its connection to the spirit and therefore not go anywhere. The body keeps us in this world, so if we think we still have one, we will continue to linger, lost or confused.

When the soul stays connected to the disembodied spirit, a same or similar consciousness to the one we had while living remains. Therefore, the spirit/entity is capable of communicating, having maintained its consciousness. If the soul manages to pass over, what sometimes gets left behind is residual "energy," whereby the emotional trauma can still be felt or experienced by local residents or investigators without any kind of intelligence being present. This is called an "imprint," and is an emotional remnant only. It can still show up as a ghost. This is the result of a highly emotional charge of energy left behind, not only from deaths that might occur, but also from major life events. An imprint results from extremely emotional situations.

A stubborn or confused soul may refuse to leave because of unfinished business or a strong human or material attachment. Any consciousness left over is due to the presence of the soul. If the soul can be made to understand that there is no longer a body keeping it here or allowing it to continue its work, it will no longer cling to the ghostly spirit. It will allow the spirit to dissolve, will free itself to the other side and, in the process, free those who have had to put up with its hauntings. Soul animates both body and spirit—without it, neither one can be experienced in an intelligent form.

We have modern "ghost busters" that come in and let the soul know that it has passed. They reassure it and provide instructions for it to pass over. These ghost busters have the newest electrical instruments that are very sensitive and can pick up the presence of these spirits. They can detect changes in electrical fields, in temperature, and can pick up visual images on sensitive frequencies and detect strange unexplained audio. These things are now commonplace in examining potential proof of the reality of ghosts. We all have a spirit; we all have a soul. If one or both should survive the body, why wouldn't we see or at least detect them on occasion? As our technology improves we find ourselves getting closer to the truth, and at a faster rate than we have ever experienced in the past.

35. Do you believe that psychic abilities like esp, psychic readings, or foretelling the future accurately are possible? Why or why not?

Yes. Many psychics exist but only a few are gifted enough to provide accurate information about you that they could have never known. I once had such a reading, leaving no doubt about the abilities of a skilled psychic. It was sometime around 1988 and my good friend, Jack Barranger, insisted I accompany him to a psychic reading. He had been to her before and assured me she was "the real deal." (I will not divulge her name since she may prefer privacy at this later date.) We drove from Los Angeles and arrived at her home in Orange County. She did not advertise her services and never had to, it was by word of mouth only and she had a steady clientele. In the reading she knew that I was not originally from California. Most people are not, so that did not impress me. Then she looked straight at me and said, "You've lived in Colorado before." That really impressed me. I spent all of 1982 in the Denver area. I had been laid off from a technical job with New Hampshire Public Television and went to Denver because cable television was just starting out and their corporate offices were there. I wanted to work more in production, so did a nine-month unpaid internship while collecting unemployment, followed by part-time production work at a small company in Boulder. It gave me the needed experience. That's why I went there – or so I thought. But she said, "You did something very important in Colorado. What was it?" I did not have to think long. On the news there were continuous stories of people getting lost in the mountains and dying of exposure. I wanted to help. I found a real live mountain man and a woman who was an expert on outdoor plants. We took production gear and headed off into the mountains for four days. I produced, shot and edited a full-length documentary on how to survive in the wilderness if you get lost, including building a shelter, how to identify edible plants, how to build a fire and stay warm, how to make fishing gear from scratch, and how to find your way out. Friends told me that this program played for many years on their public access channel after I had left Colorado. And before I had left the state, at least one call came into the station from someone saying that the program had helped to save their life. When I explained all this she said, "That's why you went there. You lost your life in the mountains of Colorado in a past life, and you had to go back there. In fact, you've had a few past lives in Colorado." I was amazed by this news. I now understood that your path in life may not unfold for reasons you may have consciously chosen, but there instead could be "unfinished business" left that needs to be resolved.

She also asked me who the singer was in my life. For the life of me I could not identify a singer that was in my life – not now or at any time in the past. She insisted, "You're working with a singer, just keep that in mind." I believe she was about to reveal more about this to me, but my confusion stopped her. During the ride home, it hit me. I felt like an idiot and kicked myself because of what she might have told me. I had written a true story screenplay about a wrongly accused person whom I knew, and was trying to market it. His last name was Singer.

Good psychic readings as experienced above are possible. Esp and foretelling the future accurately may not be as easy. I believe gifted psychics can pick up future patterns and make accurate predictions based on the time and place of the reading. But we have free will. The future is not necessarily set in stone. As soon as a psychic predicts something in your future and you then become conscious of it, you have the ability to change it. The prediction may be accurate at the time of the reading, but as soon as you become conscious of it, the prediction can change or become completely wrong depending on how one reacts to the information. This means that what you thought was a not so good reading could have actually been pretty accurate at the time.

36. Is everything really connected at some ultimate physical level? Please explain.

Yes, quantum physics has proven it and there's a revolution in science because of it. We've spent centuries breaking things down into their smallest particles, trying to figure things out, only to discover that when things are broken down as far as they can go, they're really all "One," and connected together. This also includes us. We are connected together, we are all One, and only when we start acting in ways that respect this, will we see positive change in the world.

Chapter 8
OTHER LIFE

37. Do you believe we are being visited by an advanced intelligence today? Explain if needed.

The more one looks into the subject, the more it seems certain. The vastness of the universe is virtually unfathomable. Scientists have calculated how many planets could support intelligent life based on estimated solar systems, and it's in the billions. There's an article on www.space.com that suggests 60 billion planets in our own Milky Way galaxy alone could support life. This means that out of those 60 billion with basic life, highly intelligent forms must be teeming throughout this galaxy itself, even if the percentage is small. Billions of star systems are older than ours, thereby providing the time for these life forms to grow more advanced than we are and develop space travel. Most any race capable of visiting us should also have the technology to remain hidden, should they so desire, barring any malfunctions or complications that might expose them. So yes, I believe it is happening and that many different races are likely monitoring us.

That was my "safe" answer. Beyond this I have had some interesting sightings and experiences, but will not get into any long drawn-out descriptions here. What I will say is that I grew up in a small town in western Massachusetts that had two summers of interesting UFO activity – 1967-1968. I believe the reason for this activity was that in 1960, only fifteen years after the first atomic bombs were dropped in Japan, a nuclear power plant was built across the valley from our home, on a remote mountain. It was the very first nuclear power plant in New England and only the third in the U.S. I also lived directly next to a fenced reservoir that served as one of the city's main water supplies, across the valley from this power plant. Prevailing winds carrying radiation would not necessarily settle into the valley between our mountains, but would likely carry straight across the valley to the city's water supply. I believe the strange craft I witnessed as a youth were there because they were monitoring the area's water supply and the possible effects of nuclear radiation on the surrounding community. We also had an aboveground swimming pool and I once witnessed, late at night from my bedroom window, a very small hovering disc-shaped craft that was taking water samples out of our pool with a hose-like device. It had a window that showed movement from a small shadowy figure inside (I was frozen with fear and just praying they wouldn't see me). There was another sighting with my mother that she still asks, from time to time, if I remember. Years later I put these pieces together and realized, in all likelihood, why these strange objects were there. Later in life I had another amazing experience with two people out in the Nevada desert, near Area 51, that cemented my belief in otherworldly visitations.

38. Do you believe we were visited by an advanced intelligence in the ancient past? Please explain.

One of the world's greatest proponents of this theory was the well-known author and researcher Zecharia Sitchin, whose books on this subject have sold millions worldwide and been published in over 30 languages. I was fortunate enough to have been a personal videographer of his, traveling with him to ancient sites around the world from 1996 to 1999, recording what he considered evidence before he became too old to travel. I wrote the Foreword to the 2011 book *The Legacy of Zecharia Sitchin*, by M.J. Evans, detailing more about these travels, and was the co-publisher of his 1996 book *Of Heaven and Earth* (with contributors). Having functioned as the primary means of documenting much of his evidence, I would have to agree that yes, we were influenced by some kind of outside intelligence in ancient times. I may not agree with all of his theories, but the material I do agree with was too compelling to dismiss. His book *Genesis Revisited* represents a good overview of his theories. There are also the books of Christian O'Brien, now quite rare and expensive, including *The Shining Ones* and *The Genius of the Few: The Story of Those Who Founded the Garden of Eden*, as well as William Bramley's *The Gods of Eden*, and many others. This subject has grown in popularity with the History Channels' series, Ancient Aliens, which gives viewers much to think about.

39. If it were announced that we have begun to communicate with an alien race and they may one day wish to visit us, how do you think this would affect our world and you personally?

It is often said that should such a thing occur, our society and its religious foundations would crumble. I tend to agree. I don't believe we are mature enough yet as a species to adjust our ideas smoothly in such an event. We are still further along than we once were, and I believe the day may come when we are ready – and when it does, then and only then, certain "friends" out there may suddenly turn up. They may be waiting for the day when we can expand beyond our limited, tribal-based, violent factions that claim God exclusively for their own. An advanced intelligence may not wish to be responsible for smashing this illusion and creating the obvious chaos that would result. I believe otherworldly emissaries may appear only when we have come to collectively recognize a more all-encompassing, universal God of love that includes everyone and everything, whether it be of this Earth or not.

40. If alien beings picked you up and were planning to take over the Earth, what would you say to talk them out of it? Or would you?

Before presenting my argument, the known history of expansionism on this planet would have to be considered. All explorers are primarily concerned with their own personal gain and, in the long run, are not so concerned about those who stand in their way. Those who they happen to encounter are exploited – either right away, or slowly and methodically. When the white race came to America the native peoples were badly exploited, poisoned or massacred, and when that didn't work, friendly "treaties" were employed – none of which were kept. In more recent times, the terrible concentration camp extermination of over six million Jews in the 20th Century shows that human nature is cruel and egotistical. One might argue that territorial expansion while exploiting whatever is in the path is something exclusive to the human condition, but a quick study of nature shows this could be a basic feature among many life forms – from herd animals to locusts to schools of fish to animals that run in packs – the list goes on and on. Knowing this spells trouble should any so-called "kind-hearted" aliens show up on our doorstep, ready to "help." One might argue that a higher intelligence should also have higher moral values, and we therefore should trust in that. But it has been the exact opposite on planet Earth – a higher intelligence provides those who have it with more devious means to operate. Explorers also have needs and wants, with history showing that they will usually take what others have, by guile or by force, if needed, to satisfy themselves. With all this being known, I would tell them what a mistake it has been for us to do this to each other, because it has resulted in the state of affairs we have now. However, if they would become visitors that stopped in from time to time, sharing knowledge and advice, they would become highly esteemed and respected, rather than scorned as forceful dictators should they actually take over. If they planned to wipe us out and simply take the planet, I would tell them that they would be tampering with God's plan to allow us to work out our own problems and to learn lessons for ourselves. This is our home; it is where we need to stay and do this. That would be the best I could do.

Chapter 9

PERSONAL GROWTH

41. The world's greatest philosopher, Plato, said, "Know thyself." What can you do to know yourself better?

There is an exercise called Self-Observation that likely originated from the legendary mystic, Gurdjieff. I had included a version of it in *Triumph of the Human Spirit*, but the following explanation is more clear and concise. If done consistently, it has the potential to reveal a great deal about the true Self to most anyone. Without a strong sense of the soul, most people are left with bodies that function as machines based on stimulus and response. We get trapped in this cycle. Self-Observation pulls you back from the machine-based responses enough for you to observe and *study* them. All one needs to do in order to perform this successfully is to divide one's attention. It's not as easy as it sounds, but with practice one can reap the rewards. As much possible, during the day, focus your attention outward as you normally do, but also direct part of your attention inward, focusing on your emotions, reactions and internal states. This allows you to become a silent witness to what's really happening – in essence, taking on the role of your observing soul. But now you, in addition to your soul, can become conscious of your stimulus/response reactions, which in turn can reveal 1) how you are really perceiving things, 2) how others may be viewing you, 3) what distortion or imbalances are at play, and 4) what you can do to correct them. The key is to be completely non-judgmental in the process.

42. When do you feel most at peace with yourself?

When my mind is quiet. I believe our natural spiritual selves were never meant to have a chattering mind constantly pestering us with the incessant desires of the ego. Many might say they are most at peace when doing something that relaxes them, but I could be doing anything and still be at peace as long as my mind is quiet. Once I reach this quiet state, I can keep my attention on where I believe the soul resides within the body. Once done, everything feels totally balanced and perfect. Getting there requires focusing on the breath more than the exterior world and feeding its energy into an area near the heart – where I believe the soul resides. It provides both balance and inner peace. This is an exercise I share in more detail in *Triumph of the Human Spirit* – exercise number eight in the back of the book called "Entering the Cave of the Heart." I have been doing this for over 30 years and consider it a form of conscious meditation.

43. What one book has had the most profound influence upon you and why? If it happens to be the Bible don't exclude it – but then stretch yourself, and include another one.

I've read thousands of good books and on any given day my choice could be different – but what sticks out in my mind today is *The First and Last Freedom*, by Jiddu Krishnamurti. I've recommended it to others for years. Some consider him to have been the best spiritual teacher of the 20th Century. The chapters are short but each contains a profound lesson. These lessons can transform one into a completely new and interesting way of thinking. Each chapter forced me to stop and digest the information because it was so deep and profound. I would often read one chapter each night before bed and then "sleep on" its' meaning.

44. What is your greatest joy and why?

It's being with those I love. Things change and we're not going to be here forever. Every moment that can be shared with those you love should be taken, and then appreciated to the fullest. With most of my relatives far removed, visits of any kind bring the greatest joy.

45. What is your biggest fear and what can you do to overcome it?

My biggest fear is seeing blind fanaticism dash all of the incredible spiritual progress made by humanity. Fundamentalist extremism is the complete antithesis to an awakened humanity. And it is currently spreading. Compassion and mutual respect toward each other is a by-product of our spiritual evolvement, which is unfolding beautifully in the world apart from this brutal, dogmatic, religious barbarism. As one person I don't know if I can do anything to overcome such a fear, other than point to The God Pact in hopes that more awareness of it could somehow help.

46. What is the best thing that was ever done for you by a stranger or someone who did not know you very well?

An older gentleman talked me out of quitting a job, which would have affected the rest of my life. I had moved to Los Angeles in 1985 with a technical background and degree in TV production and within a short time landed a graveyard shift running master control for a cable news network. This means I ran the board that put the programming on the air. Normally a board like this can be run solo, but this was a complex operation that required two people. The person who trained me and became the other part of my team was verbally and sometimes physically abusive. I went to the night shift manager, Seymour, a mild-mannered older gentleman. He was experiencing some of the same treatment by this bully, but could remove himself from encounters more easily than I could. His talks with the perpetrator helped for only short periods and I saw no other recourse but to quit. I was dead set on it. The bully could not be fired because few had his skill level and years of experience with the job. When I gave my resignation, Seymour made me more aware of the valuable experience I was gaining and what I could be building upon for the future. He promised to come down harder on our bully and try to make things more tolerable for both of us. It worked just enough to keep me around until I found similar work at another network and moved on. I will always remember Seymour because he took the time to talk me out of quitting, when many others would not have bothered.

47. What is the best thing you have ever done for a stranger or someone you did not know well? Why?

Place: Same news network in previous question. Time: About a month after I was convinced to keep my job. One morning after my shift there was a mandatory company meeting to attend before going home, with the arriving day crew. Changes would be announced. The excess fat was being trimmed from the company in order to save money. Before the meeting Seymour told me he would not be there because they were taking his job away. He really needed his job, no one else would hire someone his age and he didn't know what he was going to do. He was devastated. The suits all sat at the front of a long table and outlined all the new plans and procedures – one of which was to eliminate Seymour's night manager job. To them, it was no longer a necessary position. It was all done with great authority and when they wrapped it up and asked if there were any questions, there was a pause and no one said a word. Then I stood up. I told them if they let Seymour go they were eliminating the best person in the entire company. I told them I wouldn't even be there if it wasn't for him, explained how he saved my job and gave them numerous other reasons why they were making a big mistake. When I finished they said they would take what I said into consideration and the meeting ended. Immediately afterward a few people from the day shift came up to me asking things like, "Who the hell *are* you?" and "That was great! Thank you." Virtually no one knew who I was, but many loved Seymour like I did. They did give him his job back, so it goes to show that no matter what happens, stand up for what you believe.

48. What is your main goal in this life? How can you accomplish it?

My main goal is to try and make a positive difference in the world. My central ideas involving the formula for a new paradigm (*Shadow of Darkness, Dawning of Light*) and spreading peace through a larger recognition of God and our place in the universe (The God Pact) may not be seriously considered by the world anytime soon, or even at all. So I'm doing the best I can to plant seeds for these ideas, so they might come to fruition at a later time.

49. What is the most profound experience you've ever had, and why?

I experienced a spontaneous event one summer evening in Massachusetts in 1984 that changed my life forever. It allowed me more than a glimpse of another reality. At this time, I had decided to become a "born-again Christian" and to seriously explore what this had to offer. One evening after reading Numbers 19 in the Bible, I went to sleep. Shortly after falling asleep I had an out-of-body experience – but didn't know it right away. I "woke up" and couldn't breathe. It felt like seeds of some kind were filling up in my mouth and blocking my air path. I ran into the bathroom trying to breathe, and tried to spit them into the sink. As fast as I could spit them out, they continued to multiply. I then looked into the mirror. Immediately upon seeing my face, I found myself simultaneously in the back seat of my car, which began to move – and with the sudden realization that I was not in my body. I was able to view things looking only out the back window of the car as it traveled faster and faster, watching scenes from my life recede in the distance as they passed. I still wonder today why I was unable to view things in the direction the car was moving. What accompanied these images was a high-pitched sound. The volume remained constant, but the pitch became higher as the car increased in speed. Then, when the pitch became really, really high, with things moving very fast, something "popped." All of a sudden everything stopped. The last thing I recall seeing were grave stone markers rushing past the sides of the car before it all stopped. Then I found myself in a black and silent void. It was like being in space but with no stars – much like a vacuum. It was not a dream; I was fully "there" and it was like I was floating. Some time passed and I became acclimated to the surroundings (or rather, lack thereof), wondering where I was and what this was all about. Finally, from the far end of this void came an energy, from a distance, in the form of a radiating lavender color. As the waves of this energy reached me, an incredible peace accompanied this color. Then, from out of the distance appeared a Christ figure. As he approached me, I realized that this energy was coming from him. Once I could clearly see him, he radiated the most incredible, blissful peace that one could ever imagine. It radiated from him in the form of this lavender-colored energy and is by far the most awesome, beautiful feeling I believe one could ever have.

I was then transported into yet another realm that is far more vibrant and real than the current world we inhabit. I was shown things – of and by this Christ figure – with deep symbolic meaning since no words were spoken. Much was shown in symbols and super vivid "snap-shots," each meant to show something important. Some of it was easy to interpret; some of it was not. When something was important, each snapshot would "jump" or move in closer two or three times, to be sure I would remember the image. I am thankful for what I learned. There was no fluid movement in this realm; it was all shown in "pictures," but it had more richness and was far more vibrant than the world we inhabit here. When I awoke about four hours later, my bed was soaked in so much sweat that it was like a bucket of water had been dumped on me in my sleep. Although I had not yet learned what to call it, I had, at this moment, become a Gnostic. It was the most incredible event of my life.

Chapter 10

PHILOSOPHY

50. What is the purpose of life (all of life) existing on earth?

All of life is dependent on nature, and nature is a living intelligence. Therefore, the purpose of life is to support nature. All of life is part of her. She has chosen to harbor herself on this planet because its' ideal placement can support her and allow her to thrive under normal circumstances. Nature uses the sun and the planets' axis and rotation to express herself, and the conditions found on Earth are perfect for her to thrive. The purpose of life is to support nature and the purpose of nature is to support life.

51. What is the meaning of human life?

This is a question that should be seriously explored by everyone, because the meaning of human life is *not* to take the place of nature. The core purpose of life on the planet involves having a symbiotic connection with what makes it go – nature. Human life has gone astray and the condition of the planet makes that clear. It's not our job to dump sludge and nuclear waste into her oceans and waterways, make genetically modified crops, outfish the oceans, or to cause the direct extinction of millions of species that otherwise had the right to remain here, and keep nature balanced. The meaning of human life should therefore be to keep nature balanced. As a result, our home would remain safe.

52. What is the meaning of your life?

It is the soul that defines each of our lives and gives us purpose. It is therefore up to us to make contact with our souls and determine this meaning for each of us, individually. This is why there is so much confusion in the world. The vast majority of people either don't know with any certainty if they have a soul, or they simply don't know how to make contact with it in a strong enough way to make the right decisions for them personally. The meaning of my life is to tell people this fact – to wake people up to the fact they are, first and foremost, spiritual beings. Once an inner dialogue gets created with the true Self, all confusion will vanish and one may come into alignment with their purpose in life.

53. Do we have free will? Explain why or why not.

Yes, I believe we have free will. This world is far from perfect and imperfection is the testing ground for both free will and experience. Without flaws and dangers there would be no free will, choices, discoveries, experiential events, or spiritual advancement. We are here to learn lessons – lessons that can never be learned unless we are able to make choices. Our choices are not pre-determined because that would mean our lessons would already be learned. And if our lessons were already learned, there would be no point in being here.

54. What is true happiness? Does money buy it, or can you be truly happy without it?

True happiness can be found only at the center of one's being. Millions of dollars can never ransom the incessant desires of a whining ego. It will only want more. Some of the happiest people in the world run around with no shoes and little food. Often times, the more money one has, the more problems they have. And the more problems one has, the less happy one often is. Those without wealth often believe that money will solve all of their problems. And they're right. Money would solve their current problems, but it would create far more than they had to begin with! I'm not saying money is the root of all evil. What I'm saying is that money is used as a tool to support the evil tendencies of mankind. We fall prey to it too easily.

55. What is more real – mind or matter? Please give your reasons.

They are both equally real. It depends on the perspective one takes when considering the question. For example, another way to ask the question is, "If a tree falls in the forest and no one is there to hear it, does it make a sound?" This can favor either the mind or matter. From the physical perspective, one may believe the tree still makes a sound without the mind being there to process it, so matter is more real than the mind, physically. But the other perspective is from someone who believes that no sound can possibly exist *to them*, unless they are there to process it. They rely on experiential evidence in order for something to exist verifiably. So it depends on one's perspective. Tests in quantum physics shows that light can be perceived as either a particle or a wave, depending on the observer. It's the same thing. Both are equally real until the observer makes a decision.

56. Is reality just a dream? Explain why or why not.

Reality is not a dream, but the mind can fool us into believing it. One popular notion of this idea – that reality is just a dream or an illusion – is based on the Sanskrit word *maya*, which is mistakenly interpreted by some as meaning "illusion." However, maya is really a creative power rather than an illusion. In the Bhagavad-Gita (IV:6) Krishna says, "I come into being through my maya," which clearly makes it a creative force rather than a dream or illusion. There is, however, a dream-like quality to our consciousness that we experience every day. A good example of this is when you drive in your car, get to your destination and then don't remember much about getting there. One of my favorite authors, Colin Wilson, calls this the robot. It is created by the mind, not by your surroundings. The mind likes to shut down and go on automatic pilot as soon as it becomes familiar with any sort of task. This creates a world full of sleepwalkers. The great mystic and spiritual teacher, Gurdjieff, would often do crazy things in front of his students just to snap them out of their dream-like stupors. Something that jars your senses also awakens you, temporarily, and you become more alive. Reality is not a dream and your life is not meant to sleep through it.

57. If you could change one thing about the world, what would it be and why?

I would change the paradigm because this one is no longer working. I have envisioned a four-point plan that could bring about this change over a few decades, but I suppose changing the world is not on the agenda for an amateur social engineer lacking power, money or influence. I also understand that my lack of experience in world affairs exposes me to gross oversimplifications in my approach – but I still believe that much of it could function and be useful in some parts of the world.

58. If you could go back in history and witness just one event, with no way to change it and without being seen, what would it be and why?

I'd head straight back to the Garden of Eden and hang out there until the so-called serpent came along. Let's see how that whole scenario played out. The reason is that if anything of significance really did happen there, I'd be able too see how symbolic or literal the story really was, and then have a better understanding of who we really are as a result.

59. Finish this sentence and expand if you wish: Freedom is…

…being able to express your true essence. Who you really are – the soul – is covered over by material darkness and rarely shines through enough to be recognized or used properly. True freedom gives the soul room to breath and puts people on their true path.

60. Finish this sentence and expand if you wish: Love is…

…the salvation of mankind. It's here to save us if we decide to use it. It is the only thing capable of doing this because it is the most powerful force in the universe. There is only one condition needed to achieve this salvation, and that is that we use this force together.

Chapter 11
THE PLANET

61. Finish this sentence and explain why: The world needs…

…mankind to wake up. There is a clear pattern throughout history, which shows that mankind is evolving spiritually. A few great teachers that are spiritually awake can and do provide a glimpse of human potential and a more enlightened state of being that may await us. Should we be evolving in this way then a better world surely does await us. It just depends on how long this destructive paradigm we're in is allowed to hold on and prevent us from growing more fully in a spiritual and holistic direction. If we know the direction we need to go, then we need to wake up and start walking on the right path.

> God loves us: He has not worked out a design for our failure. Man has the capacity to do right as well as wrong, and his history is a path upward, not downward. The past is strewn with the ruins of the empires of tyranny, and each is a monument not merely to man's blunders but to his capacity to overcome them... progress has been made. This is why I remain an optimist, though I am also a realist about the barriers before us.
>
> —Martin Luther King, Jr.

62. What is the best thing you can commit to that will make this world a better place?

To live by the Golden Rule – treat everyone the way I would want to be treated in the same situation. I have proposed some large-scale ideas that could be helpful to the world, but am in no position to execute them to any effective degree. With this in mind, the best way to make an impact is to focus on that which you have direct control over. And what you have direct control over is each daily situation you encounter involving those you have contact with. If everyone lived by the Golden Rule, many bad situations would disappear overnight. Suffering could be diminished. By living this way, I can help to eliminate some uncomfortable situations that those closest to me might otherwise encounter.

Chapter 12

RELIGION

63. Is there one true religion? Explain why or why not.

No. There is one true God, but not one true religion. We just interpret Him differently, due to the differences in people and cultures. When we work with each other and start recognizing that there is one true God, then one true religion may start coming into place. I personally don't believe that one true religion should ever be the goal, however. If the one true God is recognized as an all-loving, non-exclusive being and the goal (of loving everyone just as God does) is the same, it really doesn't matter how one worships Him. The true God is non-exclusive and all-loving, so our religious differences need never be an issue should we share in this loving God.

64. Is heaven on earth possible? Explain why or why not.

I do not believe so. Many attempts have been made at creating a utopian society, which would be the best representation of heaven on earth. I believe that is the point in trying to create a utopia. But heaven, as I and many would like to believe, is devoid of problems. Problems are for the physical world, where opposites and conflicts arise. There is no way to avoid these in any functioning attempt at a utopian society. The closest one can get to heaven on earth is to create it in one's heart and then express it to the world, individually. It may not come out perfectly, but it's better than not trying at all.

65. Is hell a fantasy or is it real? Please explain.

The closest thing there is to hell is right here on earth. We are already spiritual beings that have come down through the depths into a very low vibration (compared to the spiritual), where fire already exists along with great suffering. There is no need for the fantasy of hell when so many people already experience those torments here. The idea of experiencing hell in an afterlife was the result of fear tactics put forth by those wishing to control others. God is an all-loving God and would not want His children to suffer eternal torments and be lost forever. That would make God sadistic and unloving toward His children. We are all His children, saints and sinners alike, and are all working our way back toward God's embrace. There are no throw-aways into some kind of demented furnace.

66. If your religion did not exist, how would you worship God?

In the same way I worship Him now. I do not use any one holy book as a strict guideline for worship, but use the best and most loving teachings from all sources that are clearly universal. Despite the claims of each separate religion, God is not exclusive to them. We are all His children. Separate religions allow us to express forms of worship that are more comfortable to different ethnic groups or those from different geographical areas. Different paths to God should be respected as long as they bring no harm to others. If God wanted there to be just one religion, He would have come down and clearly presented one book to all parts of the world simultaneously, leaving no question in the hearts and minds of men everywhere that this book – and only this one – is the one that should be used. He would never pull one isolated prophet or small group aside, and speak only to them in secret, so they could then declare to the world that this is now the one true religion. I am not saying any major religions of the world are wrong or are a lie – I'm just saying they are *outdated*. Many people do what I do and follow God's calling from within, rather than from a man-made organization. Our conceptions and experiences of God have grown in the modern world to the point where we must express them a bit differently than older forms of worship.

67. What is prayer?

Prayer is an important way to keep yourself aligned with God. Depending on the culture, prayer can be directed to not only God, but to other beings that might care for you – including spirit guides, deceased ancestors, archetypal powers, or even a lofty philosophical ideal. I pray not only to God, but to other guides or positive beings that I believe can hear me. When addressing each one at the prayer's beginning I try to "tune in" to their energy to make the proper connection. When I feel a presence or connection with all whom I have addressed, I continue with the prayer. God, of course, comes first. I believe we all have helpers, guides, a higher Self, and friends on the other side that watch us and sometimes help. Tuning in to those who care for you, even though you cannot see them, really isn't such a bad idea. Prayer keeps you aligned with everything that loves you and cares for you, should you decide to seek them out.

68. Do you believe there was a "fall of man," where an apple was eaten in the Garden of Eden, we fell from grace with God, and were expelled from paradise? If so, were these literal events or what really happened?

This is the one historical "event" I'd like to witness, as answered in a previous question. The entire nature of man's physical origin and psychological make-up could well rest on what happened here, as well as who or what both God and Satan are. Lots of questions would get answered here. So what do I believe happened? Man was in transition, being watched over while moving from a slightly lower form into something higher. Adam and Eve were the prototypes of this new "creation." The Garden of Eden is symbolic for nature because when in the Garden we were part of nature itself, living there harmoniously. This new creation ingested an apple, symbolic for the "fruit of knowledge," that opened their eyes. They became like gods, able to see both good and evil, and became embarrassed from the lack of clothes, or having a natural state. They fell from their natural state. Now apart from nature, they had to be expelled and live in a completely different way. We remain in this unbalanced state today.

Chapter 13

SCIENCE

69. What is nature?

Nature is the soul of planet Earth, expressing herself. She is a living, creative intelligence. Much the way a great painter uses the canvas, nature paints her masterpiece with living beauty. Her tapestry is interconnected on every level and the strength of her work rests on the ability of each strand to hold together. As mankind continues to eliminate these strands, pieces of the painting fall away, destroying both the beauty and function of nature, on which we depend.

70. What is time and what is its true purpose?

I will hand this one over to Aristotle, who once said, "Time is the most unknown of all unknown things." Beyond this I can only guess that it is a conductor of energy that needs physical space to operate. Without it, all forms of energy would be frozen blocks of mass that would be unable to move, or use or generate any energy. Therefore, time conducts it. Life is a process and only time, along with space, can provide the stage for the linear process of life to operate. Although we're still not sure exactly what it is, we do know that time is our most important tool. It's easy to use, but easy to waste. Its' purpose is to allow things to flow through the physical world and express what they truly are. It is often said that all we have is time, so we must use it as wisely as possible.

71. What is consciousness?

I believe consciousness to be the foundational basis of the Universe. All of humanity, collectively, shares in the primary consciousness of God. In that respect, we, in fact, are God. We just don't know it yet. Those entrenched in religious dogma will consider this statement blasphemy, but an interesting and credible scientific theory has emerged that recognizes consciousness as the main component of the universe rather than matter. The first to propose this theory from a quantum scientific standpoint, rather than a purely mystical one, was Amit Goswami, Ph.D., in his 1993 book *The Self-Aware Universe*. Modern New Age thought claims that everything is connected. If this is the case, what is it that serves as the connecting principle? It could be consciousness. Quabalist and Biblical scholar Carlo Suares once said that the universe is spirit that is becoming self-aware by projecting from itself a cloud of consciousness upon which it can self-reflect. I fully agree.

In the old Hermetic books, which are more mystical than scientific, Hermes states that God holds everything within Himself as thought—and the entire cosmos itself is a thing composed of consciousness. These ideas are not new and revolutionary. They compose some of the oldest and wisest mystical teachings the world has ever known—the only thing new about them is that they are being rediscovered, sometimes with advanced scientific backing.

Since we are all conscious beings, we share in this connection to God. We remain unaware of this "God-consciousness" because the vast majority of us are not ready for it and it is therefore operating at an unconscious level. Our search for true meaning is right in front of us, but because the consciousness of God has been scattered out into creation and shared, we fail to comprehend it individually (except in rare cases). God is not only observing though us, but experiencing what becomes of a perfect wholeness when it becomes fragmented. This consciousness is exploring all of the options of what it truly can be and what

God's potential is. That is, in fact, who and what we really are. Remaining as a stagnant ball of perfect, unfulfilled energy was not God's purpose. People wonder why we are here, who we are, and where we are really going. The answer is that we, in fact, are God. Collectively. From an individual perspective we are blind to this fact, but from a collective sense— which an individual's consciousness cannot normally reach—the answers are clear. When we collectively realize our true identity we will immediately begin to act accordingly. This realization is a major component in the development of a holistic world view. Our collective link to God can create a better world through large-scale unity, with everyone involved.

72. In a human being, when does consciousness begin?

Many scientific studies have been made to try and determine this, with most of them concluding that consciousness begins while a baby is still in the womb. Some reports say around six months, so this is not a question about when physical life begins, but about the later development of consciousness. Scientific approaches base this on the development of required nerves for the brain to fire conscious signals properly, etc. I believe, however, that our consciousness is always there. For example, certain consciousness-expanding breathwork techniques have reportedly allowed participants to recall, and even re-live, ones' own birth (like Holotropic Breathwork, developed by Stanislav Grof, and Rebirthing, developed by Leonard Orr). If true, then consciousness has been within us from birth – or even before. It is a feature of our soul, and the form of consciousness carried by the soul is not exactly the same that we exhibit outwardly. Consciousness as we know it must certainly begin and develop. But there's a higher form that is always with us, in the background.

73. If everything evolved from amoebas in the distant past, why does the world still have them?

This shows that a vital foundation to life exists in the form of amoebas. They have survived through everything. Should a major catastrophe occur, the surviving amoebas could start the evolutionary process over again. This is something a major designer or creator would be sure to have in place, being vital to the structure of life. You cannot have a bridge and continue to travel over it without having the foundation still present.

74. Where do thoughts come from?

As one grows and cognition appears, thoughts also appear in relation the level of cognition that is developed. Our cognition interacts with our feelings, surroundings and experiences to create an ego or identity, which in turn creates most of our everyday thoughts. This ego is primarily concerned with its own self-gratification and survival, as well as building its own identity into something important. As one grows, one starts accepting this identity as the real "you." This ego is where your thoughts come from, but *it is not you*. Zen masters have said that the mind is a trap, but the mind is not a trap in itself – it creates a nest for the ego, which is the thing that traps you. The ego sometimes creates selfish or crazy-sounding thoughts that seem to come from nowhere because again, it is not the real you. The ego presents itself using the "chattering monkey mind," that is only concerned with its desires. There is a bumper sticker that says, "Don't believe everything you think." In other words, the ego is crazy. There is also a popular metaphysical notion going around that claims that thoughts from the collective consciousness are floating around out there, something like bubbles, and when one resonates with you, it can jump inside your head and surprise you. This isn't so. The mind is very deep and complex; there are many layers and they all belong to you. Aside from the ego being hard-wired into the mind, there is a higher Self that can come through – not as standard thought, but through intuition. This can then be processed into thought, and provide you with guidance. The soul, the real you, is always there but remains in the background as an observer. The nicest people are better at pushing the ego aside and allowing the soul to shine through. The ego handles ones' survival so must take precedence in this world. It is not often as nice or loving as the soul, or the real you, which we are learning to make better contact with.

75. Why is the Universe so incredibly large, where does it end, and what do you believe its purpose is?

The Universe is so large because it's expanding at the speed of light ever since the Big Bang occurred 13.8 billion years ago. No one knows where it ends or if it really does end. The only discernible purpose scientists have encountered is replication – the Universe spawns smaller, baby universes (with the help of black holes) that are slightly different from the "parent." This could be providing the basis for the laws of nature to occur not only on Earth, but throughout the Universe. The Universe is geared toward replication and of course expansion, but that only tells us what it's doing. We still don't know why it's doing this with any certainty. My opinion is that before the Big Bang, God was a conscious and complete entity, compressed as this pre-Big Bang entity. He was a pure but unrealized consciousness. I believe that consciousness, not matter, is the foundational substance of the Universe. Because it is expanding, God's consciousness is expanding and therefore, our consciousness (in a collective sense) is doing the same. Each person and being with consciousness reflects the creator in a holographic sense – we all have the consciousness of God within us. For the Universe itself to be involved in replication requires, at least to me, the involvement of a conscious intelligence. The Big Bang may have occurred because God wished to realize His own consciousness through movement and experience. We are expressions of God's consciousness and the entire Universe is a reflection of this. If the Universe did not have a purpose, we would not have a purpose. And our purpose seems to be clear – human consciousness is expanding, much like the Universe is. We are growing and learning; we are beginning to rise above our animal natures to realize the Godly part of us. As God realizes His own consciousness throughout the Universe, through myriad ways of experience, we are also doing the same – being tied inexorably to Him as holographic souls that are really all One.

Chapter 14

THE SOUL

76. What is the human soul?

The soul is the innermost part of us, the core of our being. It is the very essence of who we are and is described as an inner light by cultures throughout the world. The human soul is made up of light. God is also composed of this same light. This is why many claim that we are all part of God. We all hold within us a small spark of God and therefore, each of us has a "Godly" nature. Ever since I was a child, I've been able to see a highly luminous, brilliant light within my field of vision, which became harder to see as I grew older. I developed an exercise to bring it back, as found in my book *Triumph of the Human Spirit*, which shows and describes what it looks like, along with historical references to the soul being composed of light, and my personal views on its function. In short, and echoing Gnostic phraseology, we all have a spark of divinity within us. There is a Gnostic story that relates how these divine sparks have become trapped in matter. While here, we must work at growing spiritually to the point where we can return to our true home with God. This physical realm operates on a low and dense vibration. Spiritual pursuits help us to raise our vibration and grow in ways that might assist us in reaching our true home. The human soul is who we really are, and we are here to express it as best we can. We enter the world with it and it provides the basic blueprint for each individual personality. When we leave the world we take it with us – changed, hopefully for the better – by our choices and experiences here.

> When I die, my deeds will follow along with me – that is how I imagine it. I will bring with me what I have done. In the meantime it is important to insure that I do not stand at the end with empty hands.   —Carl Jung

77. What is the difference between the soul and spirit?

The soul is the innermost part of us, the core of our being. It is the very essence of who we are and is described as an inner light by cultures throughout the world. It is what comes here from that other place from which we came. And it is what will return. It carries our life imprint with it when it leaves, and functions while here as a certain form of consciousness. I have taught those who are sensitive enough on how to view their own soul – to actually see it within their field of vision and experience it – and some have succeeded.

The spirit is different – it is a nonmaterial, humanlike form. It is an energy field that surrounds the body, which is, for example, the thing that accounts for out of body experiences and, if a traumatic death should occur, a ghost or spirit. Everyone has a spirit body for a short time after one passes. But this spirit body dissipates once the soul ascends back home, to where it must return, thereby no longer animating the spirit body. The soul – the real you – survives bodily death. When one understands what a spirit and a soul really are, it becomes clear that the way we use the term "spiritual" is a misnomer of sorts. When one becomes conscious of his or her soulful nature, the term "spiritual" is often used. We discuss our "spiritual nature," or call ourselves "spiritual beings." But we are actually soulful beings. Being spiritual is an expression of our soulful natures. Spirituality is a general term used to express our soulful natures.

78. Where does the soul reside?

From my own experience and research I believe that the soul resides in the chest, nestled near the heart and between the lungs. The reason is because I have seen, from a young age, an extremely luminous part of me that I believe is the soul. My breath energizes it and expands it, making it shine more brightly. The ancient Greek word *pneuma* means "breath," but it also means "soul." It has a double meaning. In the Old Testament the Hebrew word *nephesh* was used for soul, which comes from the verb "to breathe." The ancients knew exactly what they were talking about. The soul needs the breath to stay in the body – once you stop breathing and pass away, the soul knows to move on. While we are alive, the breath goes into the lungs. Blood comes from the right side of the heart and passes through the lungs, picking up the oxygen molecules, then goes into the left side of the heart. I believe the soul may reside at the transfer point of oxygen-energized blood, somewhere between the lungs and the left side of the heart. I strongly believe the soul resides somewhere in this area – not as a physical object, but as a small and hidden "spark." This would be the perfect place for it to be energized by the breath – and is also the place where I have "felt" its presence.

79. Do animals have souls? What makes you believe this?

Of course they do. It is arrogant to believe that only humans have souls. When you really get to know an animal, really know them, it's clear they have a soul just like you do. It just happens to be smaller. Pound for pound, however, many animals have souls larger than human ones. Love is the primary by-product and expression of the soul. Animals give so much love and pure expression of their souls, there is absolutely no question that they have them.

Chapter 15

SPIRITUALITY

80. What is the difference between spirituality and religion?

Religion and spirituality are two different things, and thinking they are the same has caused countless problems for humanity in the past. Because of the struggle for religious power there has been little room in the past for spiritual freedom. Religion is prone to fanaticism, and has sometimes tried to force beliefs onto others. No one should use force, even in subtle ways, to obtain followers. As we grow, spiritually, we sometimes wander outside the boundaries of our religion. Yet, when we follow our spiritual insights, we often know that we are right no matter what any religious guru or scientific fact sheet could tell us. The best definition I've heard for religion comes from William James who calls it, "the feelings, acts and experiences of individual men in their solitude, so far as they apprehend themselves to stand in relation to whatever they may consider the divine." The key words here are "in their solitude." Most people consider religion to be a group thing—that is how the churches view it and would like us to view it. They don't function well with their believers in solitude. What James, I believe, really identifies here is spirituality. There is a big difference between spirituality and religion. There's an old saying that says, "Religion is for the masses, while spirituality is for the individual." If this is true, then James has defined spirituality, not religion. Note also in his quote the use of the words "individual men."

James is defining what religion *should* be, not what it is. Religion should be an inner, spiritual quest – but ever since it became "organized," it has lost its solitude and the answers which that solitude brings. Even with knowing the importance of solitude, many still go to church, are told what to believe and make no effort to experience God for themselves. I am not saying one should give up church if they happen to attend. What I am encouraging is the experience of the human spirit. We put faith over experience – and cling to it because it's easier, it takes no considerable effort to have faith. But it is killing us on a deep and important level. Our spirits have been neglected and wounded. We must learn how to heal. We must make efforts to *experience* God. Religion, in general, contains many concepts, while spirituality centers around experience. The concepts of religion will not save you. If you come to this Earth and do little with the soul, allowing it to stagnate because you have "faith," or have simply accepted a savior into your life, your soul will not grow, it will suffer. It will suffer without your *active cooperation*. Part of your mission in life, whether it be conscious or unconscious, is to nurture and strengthen the soul; it is why you are here. If your soul were perfect, there would be no need to be here.

The word religion provides a clue to humanity's real goal and purpose. What does it really mean? All societies have and cherish religion, but we have gotten away from the true meaning of the word. The Latin word, *Religio*, has two components: *re*, meaning again or afresh, and *ligio*, indicating a binding or tying together. So religion is basically the attempt by humankind to *renew* its bond to God. This implies that we're trying to get back something we once had at an earlier time – which is a closer connection to God.

We are spiritual beings who have a spiritual home, away from here, and closer to God. We were there at one time, and must now find our way back. To re-bind something back together, or tie something together again, implies work and effort more than faith or belief. Therefore, what religion was intended to be, spirituality has become.

81. Do you believe that you have a Higher Self, a greater and wiser part of you that observes your life from afar? If so, what makes you believe this?

Yes, I believe we all have a Higher Self and it is with you always. It has great wisdom, bears witness to your deeds – and even records them. It may try to contact you at times for the greater good of all or the betterment of yourself, through what's often called that still, small voice. I believe this because I am sometimes in contact with my Higher Self. It has taken years of learning how to listen, and I am by no means an expert, but I do believe this Higher Self exists and it is possible to align oneself with it.

82. Finish this sentence and explain why: I'm fully in the present moment when...

...I'm writing. It's the thing I enjoy the most, so it naturally follows that a full engagement of my attention while doing this blocks out any memories of the past, or anticipations of the future. The present moment is all there is whenever one is engaged in what they love.

83. Finish this sentence and expand if you wish: Darkness is...

...the foundational negative polarity in our dualistic world. Opposites are needed for reality to function, and darkness rules the polar negative. There is a Gnostic story of Light and Darkness, which says the universe was created with these two inherent principles being present from the start. The Light was eternal and therefore not bothered by the coexisting Darkness. But the Darkness contained internal conflict. This conflict outwardly manifested as a desire to attack and capture the Light. After a major battle was fought between them, it resulted in the intermingling of Darkness and Light. This created the physical worlds of matter (Darkness), with our souls or spirits (the Light) being trapped here. Whenever the soul is removed or rises above matter, the body dies. The soul lives on as a particle of light, but does not ascend fully out of its trap. While enmeshed in the physical world, we forget who we really are and how we got here (see *The Hymn of the Pearl*). The Light and Darkness are intermingled within this huge cosmos and we are part of it. We have, within ourselves, a mixture of the Light and Dark—bringing opposites like good and evil. Each of us wage this battle on a daily basis. According to the story, we must work our way out of the darkness and purify ourselves in order to find our way back home. Coming to this realization and doing something about it could be why we are here.

> *The Body is but the dark lantern, the Soul or Spirit is the Candle of the Lord that burns in it.* —John Ray

84. Finish this sentence and expand if you wish: Light is...

...the crowning positive in our dualistic system. Opposites are needed for reality to function, and light rules over the positive end of the spectrum. We are all beings of light that have been intermingled with Darkness, thereby creating opposites. It is by using these opposites that we learn, grow, help others, or overcome problems. Our lights shine more brightly when we succeed in doing this, thereby bringing us closer in our individual journeys back to God.

85. Finish this sentence and add more if you wish: Compassion is...

...love in action. The best way to see what love is is to witness a compassionate act.

86. Do you believe in the collective unconscious – where certain structures or archetypes of the unconscious are common to us all, to the point where we may be sharing some kind of divine or world mind? If yes, please elaborate.

Yes, there are powerful archetypes at work in our collective unconscious minds. The great depth psychologist Carl Jung was able to elaborate on these archetypes and their meanings better than anyone. Important "themes" of life have energies – something like a blueprint. These are archetypes. Jung understood how the mind really works and how they can influence our lives. The most important archetypes are often found in our mythological stories. The archetypes can inspire certain behaviors that we would have otherwise not understood or been able to explain. They "live" in the collective unconscious, so are common to us all.

87. How do you stay "awake?"

There are two levels to this. There is being "awake" when one is fully engaged in the present moment, when only the "now" exists. This usually occurs when one is involved in something they are passionate about. Remaining in this awakened state of mind, for me, requires staying passionate about the task at hand. That's all it usually takes. The highest level of being awake involves the experience of an enlightened state, when kundalini energy has risen up through the spine and one is transformed into a higher level of consciousness. When this happens one is totally and completely awake. Only the greatest spiritual masters are able to maintain this level of consciousness for any reasonable period of time – and I don't know how they do it.

88. Finish this sentence and add more if you wish: Enlightenment is...

...the direct experience of the actual part of God that is within you. It is a union of sorts—some would term it a "reunion." One finds their wholeness with God, which is a transformative experience. A certain genius or new way of being unfolds from within those who have awakened, giving hope for the future. Instead of this occurring in rare isolated events, it could one day be common among us all. It shows that mankind does indeed have the potential to transform into something that will be more fully conscious. Since we are learning that we are truly "One," this could happen in a collective sense. As a result, there is hope for world peace and the reversal of the damage we have done to each other and the planet. It may still be far in the future, but it remains a clear possibility. Should we decide to get crazy and actually work toward this specific goal, there's a chance we could transform sooner.

89. Are we being guided as a species to an ultimate destination? If so, explain whom or what is guiding us, and what the destination might be.

Yes, we are being guided. This is one of the major ideas that I strongly believe in. When one looks at the larger historical picture, a pattern of spiritual growth and maturity within mankind seems to be taking place. In general, we are not so brutal and bloodthirsty as in the past, but are developing more awareness, kindness and compassion. Despite the mess we have made of the world, there really is hope for mankind.

We are all part of God and it is that Godly part of us that is providing the guidance. We are not alone on this journey because our individual consciousness is also part of God's consciousness. This entire consciousness that we are part of is in the process of experiencing every possible variation of life and activity in order to define Its' totality. It is clear that we are playing a major role in God's own self-realization. This role is what is guiding us. We may ask, "If God is all powerful, why does he need his own self-realization?" If we go back to what God may have been before the Big Bang, which is rather hard to imagine, it seems that it would be an extremely boring existence to just "be." Nothing physical would be there. It would be a fullness with no action or existence, without knowing what existence would be like or could be. I believe that an all-powerful God would want to use that power. That is what is being played out right here and now. Once that power has been made manifest through us, in every conceivable possibility and experience, I think there would be some kind of tremendous benefit involved at the end. Time, space and movement are required to accomplish this task, of which this dualistic system is composed. God is One, but has fragmented Itself into darkness & light, matter & spirit, good & evil, and all forms of opposites via the Big Bang. His consciousness is exploring itself, away from the compressed Oneness that had no activity, which was nothing more than a powerful, beautiful, but stagnant wholeness.

God's consciousness needed a wide variety of conscious entities to accomplish Its' defining task, and mankind holds the key position. The key for God Himself to return from this dualistic reality is for us, his consciousness, to collectively reach the realization of Oneness and our identity with God. God cannot magically pull His consciousness back together after it has been fragmented in such a way. The consciousness *itself* must do the work, and move past the illusion. For example, we must understand that when we hurt others we only hurt ourselves. Any independent, greedy action has its eventual consequence, which will surface and impact its originator with the same negative energy that spawned it. This general lesson must be learned by all. Indicators show that the conscious choices we make are leading us to something. What we do with our consciousness, in a collective sense, is the most important aspect of what is being played out in the world today. Yes, we are being guided to a destination. The idea that we are all part of God is becoming more provable with each passing day.

Chapter 16
WHAT I CAN TEACH

90. What one piece of advice would you offer to a newborn infant?

If you treat your mistakes like friends instead of enemies your wisdom will increase dramatically.

91. What advice would you give to your younger self?

Be aware that being free before you have earned it comes with a cost. Your many fascinations, wonderments and explorations of the world will rob you of success unless you can focus clearly on a goal and develop discipline in achieving it.

Chapter 17

WHAT I'VE LEARNED

92. Who have been your greatest spiritual teachers, and why?

I have never had the opportunity to sit at the feet of a master and learn anything through first-hand contact. My teachers have taught me through books and speeches, followed by my execution of principles or exercises that they passed on, which had resonated with me. With that said, the most influential teachers in my life have been J. Krishnamurti, Muktananda, Alan Watts, Mahatma Gandhi, Osho, Gopi Krishna, George Gurdjieff, Wayne Dyer and Dr. Martin Luther King, Jr.

 J. Krishnamurti is able to shift one's mode of thinking into a foreign but beautiful place that makes perfect sense, while pointing out how insane and out of balance our normal minds really are. He brings spiritual sanity into being. From his descriptions, Muktananda has seen the same inner light that I have seen and provided me with more insights into what it is and how to "use" it. Alan Watts clarifies the human condition, who we really are and how to cope with the world's shortcomings as well as anyone. His books truly opened my eyes. Mahatma Gandhi's wisdom was unparalleled and studying his views should be essential reading for everyone. Osho, formerly known as Bhagwan Shree Rajneesh, was at one point, the most awakened individual on the planet. His earlier work as Rajneesh impressed me most, before he started acquiring his large fleet of cars and falling into other distractions. Gopi Krishna's books describe how he became awakened through the power of kundalini, showing what it's like and what mankind may one day develop into. Gurdjieff can be difficult to read, but the more one studies him the larger the reward. Patience is required, but the man was a spiritual giant among giants. Wayne Dyer because he really gets it. One can see a spiritual evolvement in his life and work. Having started out as a best-selling self-help author, he has graduated into the most important themes of personal and spiritual growth, outlining them perfectly for the masses to comprehend. He is a joy to read. Dr. Martin Luther King, Jr. showed me the power of the human spirit. In the spring of 1968 it was decided that our 5th grade class would do speeches in the auditorium in front of the whole school. Most of the children presented a little poem or book excerpt. I chose a large ending portion of M.L. King's "I Have a Dream" speech. He had been assassinated a few weeks earlier and everything in his original speech moved me and made more sense to me than anything I had ever heard. I could not understand why anyone would want to kill such a great man. And the way he presented the speech touched something deep within me – it lit my spiritual fire for the first time on a very deep emotional level. The country was still shocked and hurting from the tragedy and I didn't want anyone to forget what he had said. It was my first time in front of a microphone and I gave this speech in the same style and cadence that he did. I used the microphone to its fullest ability and poured out the words with the same passion that he once did. Before it was over, one of the teachers was sobbing uncontrollably. A few other students and teachers were crying and my voice began to crack from emotion. But I made it to the end and received a tremendous applause. An eleven year-old white kid from Massachusetts, along with his little school, now understood that something so powerful exists within us that it defines our very essence. I also learned that the most beautiful, accomplished souls are the biggest threat to those who know nothing about them.

93. What is the best advice you were ever given?

Never let others make any decisions for you as long as you're capable of making them for yourself.

94. Finish this sentence and explain your reasons: I believe...

...nothing until I experience it. I believe nothing can be known with any certainty until it is *experienced*. Otherwise it is hearsay. We are all standing neck deep in the River of Truth, where we observe our surroundings and interpret what we believe to be true with our limited senses. It is deep enough to fool many into thinking this provides our truths. But in order to really know the Truth, the River must sweep you away. Life's purpose, like with the River, is to *flow*. One must experience this flow and see below the generic surface. And there are those standing neck deep in the River of Truth preaching in the name of religion about what your *ultimate Truth* should be — but they often don't know it for themselves. They are spreading hearsay or, at most, trying to relate something that is beyond words. You will not experience your Truth from these people. Only the River gives it. Religions may point out the River's path, which is good, but only you can be taken by its current. It is a powerful and personal experience. Do not accept blindly what others claim as truth, which makes you nothing more than a bystander. That is not why you are here. Your ultimate Truth awaits you in the *experience*. It is not found in the mere words of others. With such an experience, you may find what religions have been trying to provide for centuries. It will be felt within you.

95. Finish this sentence and expand if you wish: If life is a school, I have learned...

...that it's not a competition like man-made schools. No one wins unless we all win.

96. What's the lesson that has taken you the longest to learn?

Not to be so independent. We all need each other to succeed but I've always been stubborn and try doing everything myself. No man is an island, as they say, and this is a lesson I am still learning.

97. Finish this sentence and explain why: I am most grateful for...

...this one moment, here and now. It is the one tangible thing that can be grabbed onto and made the most of. At any given moment you have the power to soar.

98. What is the one thing you know for sure?

Change will always come. Some changes can be predicted more accurately than others, but no matter what, nothing can be set in stone with one hundred per cent certainty. The only thing we can know with complete certainty in this world is that change is always coming. The rest is a mystery.

99. Finish this sentence and explain why: The main lesson humanity needs to learn is...

...that we are here to help one another through compassion and mutual respect. The reason is because we are, without question, all in this together. There is no "us and them." It's just us. We must find the best way to achieve this realization so that a new paradigm, fueled by compassion and mutual respect, may unfold.

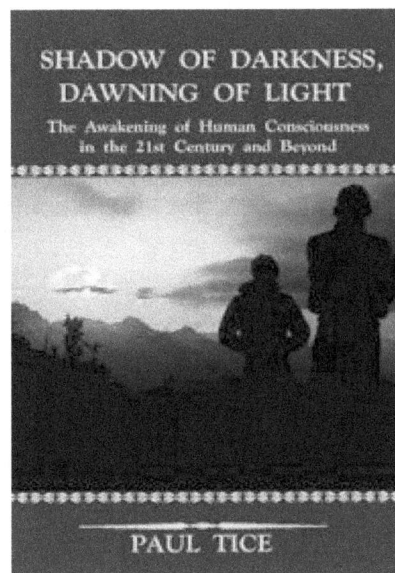